PLANNING FOR RESEARCH

SAGE HUMAN SERVICES GUIDES, VOLUME 50

D1219753

SAGE HUMAN SERVICES GUIDES

A series of books edited by ARMAND LAUFFER and CHARLES D. GARVIN. Published in cooperation with the University of Michigan School of Social Work and other organizations.

A **SAGE** HUMAN SERVICES GUIDE **50**

PLANNING FOR RESEARCH

A Guide for the Helping Professions

Raymond M. BERGER
Michael A. PATCHNER

Published in cooperation with the University of Michigan School of Social Work

SAGE PUBLICATIONS
The International Professional Publishers
Newbury Park   London   New Delhi

For information address:

SAGE Publications, Inc.
2455 Teller Road
Newbury Park, California 91320

SAGE Publications Ltd.
6 Bonhill Street
London EC2A 4PU
United Kingdom

SAGE Publications India Pvt. Ltd.
M-32 Market
Greater Kailash I
New Delhi 110 048 India

Printed in the United States of America

Library of Congress Cataloging-in-Publication Data

Berger, Raymond M. (Raymond Mark), 1950-
    Planning for research.

    (A Sage human services guide ; v. 50)
    Published in cooperation with the University of Michigan
School of Social Work.
    1. Social service—Research—Methodology. I. Patchner,
Michael A. II. Title. III. Series.
HV11.B465   1988   361'.0072   87-17535
ISBN-0-8039-3033-X (pbk.)

91 92 93 94 10 9 8 7 6 5 4 3 2

CONTENTS

FOREWORD

What a peculiar minuet social work practice and social work research have danced, sometimes reservedly bowing at a distance, occasionally joining hands in ardor, as they execute their assigned functions.

Since the meetings of the "Section on Social Economy" (1874-1879) of the American Social Science Association, research and practice in social work have been trying to make a fit in the applied science of social work. Early demonstrations of the peaks of that periodic practice-research courtship were displayed with Dr. Amoa Griswold Warner's *American Charities: A Study in Philanthropy and Economics* of 1894, and with the Pittsburgh Survey of 1909, and Mary Richmond's *Social Diagnosis* in 1917.

The necessity for this relationship gained increasing intellectual recognition in social work over the years. It was evidenced in the organization of the Social Work Research Group in 1949, the Hollis-Taylor (1951) report on *Social Work Education in the United States*, the comprehensive *Curriculum Study* (1959; Volume IX) of the Council on Social Work Education, the National Association of Social Worker's periodic research review volumes from 1959-1978, each step enhancing the quality of the practice-research relationship.

But, organic integration has never been consummated. The flirtation was interrupted by the intervention of the antiintellectualism and the professional masochism of the 1960s. The dichotomous argument regarding social work as an art versus a science obscures honest intentions. The emphasis on clinical training for privatization of social services tends to squeeze out the research ideology in the educational curricula. Underlying these barriers is the traditional dependence on research from other disciplines and the social sciences.

Fortunately, the NASW publication of Social Work Abstracts since 1965 and its expansion into the Social Work Research & Abstracts (1977), was supported by a cadre of dedicated researchers, who kept aflame the practice-research romance. They even charted a future betrothal for the social work profession in NASW's national research conference publication, the *Future of Social Work Research.*

Most of the social work researchers currently have been isolated to academic settings, which may be a commentary on the scientific commitment of social agencies and, at the same time, explain why at least a quarter of the research is investigating social workers and their education. Those academicians, fortunately, continue to serenade practitioners with the reproductive advantages of a research liaison.

A recent, and singularly positive, note was struck by the NASW's Bartlett "Practice Effectiveness" Project in the early 1980s, which uncovered more than 1,800 research studies on social work practice in the United States. Whether they will be examined or utilized will be another measure of the profession's commitmment to a scientific base for practice.

Fundamental to these oscillations in the profession has been the problem of how, and to what degree, to inculcate research attitudes and knowledge into the fiber of the developing social work professional.

The literal translation of the methodology and technique of the social sciences into the relationship methodology of social work, the misapplication of conventional physical sciences techniques to the studies of moving human targets and the complexities of social phenomena, often have created unscalable barriers for students. Even more saddening, they have tended to fixate previous mathematical and methodological traumas.

In research methodology, the social work profession faces the future with an instrument in its hand that has tended to rust, which has been only occasionally brightened in battle on behalf of the social services. Psychological research explores the capabilities of the individual, while sociology explores facts of societal functioning. Too little exploration has taken place in the interaction between those two, the complications of cause and effect in the individual-societal interaction.

This publication takes a giant step for social work kind. It gently grasps the academic proselytes by the hand and leads them step by step, converting a jungle into an orderly English garden. The adherence to the language of the Commona in explanations and the illustrations of practical social service situations makes *Planning for Research* and

Implementing the Research Plan the instruments of preference for social work students and research-deprived practitioners.

Berger and Patchner have choreographed a modern ballet of social work research, combining the classical integrity of statistical techniques with the modern problems of planning and implementation, a kind of social worker's "Rodeo." Its functional nature promises to open eyes and minds to new intellectual sensations, the forerunner of both enjoyment and achievement.

These are practical volumes that make research methodology understood. They have the promise of breaking the fear barrier and developing a positive attitude of research inquiry in the eventual day-to-day practitioner. One hopes their use and application will encourage both research and practice colleagues to work harder at achieving a sounder integration of theory and practice in social work.

—Chancey A. Alexander,
ACSW, CAE

PREFACE

Ask any group of beginning human service or social work students to name the one course that causes them the greatest anxiety, and they are likely to name research methods. That is why we have written *Planning for Research* and its companion text, *Implementing the Research Plan*.

Many students dread their research methods course and hope to get through it as quickly as possible. This is unfortunate. The helping professions rely increasingly on research-based knowledge, and an understanding of how this knowledge was developed is important for all helping professionals. Even if you are never called upon to digest the results of a research study, serious attention to research methods will serve you well: Its systematic and logical approach will teach you critical thinking. Ultimately it will help you to better understand the complex world around you.

A variety of factors account for the trepidation with which most students approach this material. We wrote this book to remedy one of the most important of these factors: the absence of a simple, easy-to-read text—a guide for helping professionals. When we were graduate students there were no research methods texts written specifically with the social worker or human service worker in mind. We had to rely on textbooks from psychology and sociology. Today there are several research methods textbooks written for social work and human service, but these books tend to be too complex, too detailed, or they focus on only one aspect of social science research methodology.

Why doesn't someone write a textbook that presents just the essentials, and does so in a complete, yet concise and easy-to-read way? As research instructors we often pondered this question. Then we decided to use our collective experience of teaching research methods to undergraduate and graduate students in the helping professions (a combined experience of over twenty years) to write just such a text.

Our goal in this work and in its companion volume, *Implementing the Research Plan: A Guide for the Helping Professions* (Sage Human Services Guide 51), has been to distill essential information about research methods into manageable proportions and then to present it concisely. We have tried throughout to stick to the basics, using simple language and lots of short examples.

Should a beginning-level research methods course teach you to be a *producer* of research, or simply an informed *consumer?* We can't answer that question here. Our texts will certainly make you a critical consumer: You will know enough to intelligently understand and critique most research studies. As a producer of research you will probably need further knowledge or the guiding hand of an expert. But our text will provide you with an excellent foundation for this task.

This book, *Planning for Research,* provides the theory and methodology for setting up your research study. It presents a review of the philosophical underpinnings of social science research through a discussion of the scientific method, and then it systematically builds a knowledge base of basic research terms. After showing how to research the literature and how to define a researchable problem, it presents a "how-to" approach for collecting a sample and selecting a research design.

Implementing the Research Plan is the companion text that was designed to be read along with this book. It discusses sources of data such as questionnaires, interviews, and available materials and provides reviews of measurement theory and instrument reliability and validity. The data analysis chapter is an attempt to familiarize the reader with the basics of data analysis and presentation. This chapter also provides an overview of statistical hypothesis testing and a comparison of the most commonly used statistical tests in the social sciences. Emphasis is on conceptual rather than computational understanding.

In today's "high-tech" world, the reader who is not familiar with computer uses will find that the chapter on computers in this companion text provides a basic understanding of computer functions and an overview of the most common types of software for a variety of uses. The placement of our chapter on ethics at the end of *Implementing the Research Plan* does not mean we think that research ethics is unimportant. Rather, it reflects our belief that social science research ethics can be understood only after the reader has a firm understanding of research principles. Appendices to *Implementing the Research Plan* provide concise frameworks for preparing a research proposal and critiquing a research study.

There is something else we have learned after many years of teaching: Those students who have confidence in their ability to master this material will have the best experience in their research course.

A positive attitude will also help if you are a practicing professional using this text to refresh old learning, or to guide you in the conduct of a research study. If you are like the many practitioners to whom we have spoken, you may think, "I can't remember anything I learned about research back in school." If that is the case, this text will be especially valuable to you. Its brevity is an asset, given your busy schedule.

You may feel at times that the understanding simply won't come. Just remember—if you have been admitted to a research course, if you are a practicing professional, in short, if you've come this far—that is proof positive you've got what it takes to learn everything in these two volumes. So don't be discouraged if the concepts seem at first to be strange or confusing. Some of them are. Know that this and its companion volume and a good dose of patience are all you need to accomplish the task.

—Raymond M. Berger
Long Beach, California

—Michael A. Patchner
Urbana, Illinois

Chapter 1

RESEARCH AND
THE SCIENTIFIC METHOD

Since the early beginnings of the human service professions, concerned individuals have responded to a myriad of social needs. We have developed programs and provided services to the poor, mentally ill, handicapped, children, the elderly, and many others. Great strides have been made in the development and delivery of services, yet most would argue that much remains to be done. We need to know more about individuals, families, groups, and communities in order to meet their needs effectively.

Research has made a significant contribution in addressing a variety of human problems. For example, research showed that many persons institutionalized for mental illness can live and function fairly well in the community provided that adequate mental health and support services are available to them (Joint Commission, 1961; President's Commission, 1978). Research has also demonstrated that prenatal care is vital to the health and well-being of new born babies (Schuster & Ashburn, 1980).

Researchers have also shown that welfare payments have not kept pace with inflation and, with the recent budget cuts, many people have been terminated from welfare programs (Aldous, 1986; Jirovec, 1984). This has caused many individuals and families to go hungry. Because of these findings social service organizations, churches, and private charities have increased their efforts to aid those who are unable to buy food for themselves or their families.

Many societal myths have been challenged by research. For example, it was generally believed that old people became senile. But research has demonstrated that senility is not an inevitable part of growing older (Baltes & Labouvie, 1973).

In another instance, society believed that nearly all people on welfare were cheaters. Again, research has shown that only a small minority of public aid recipients deliberately cheat (Julian & Kornblum, 1983; Stein, 1969; U.S. Congress, 1972). These examples illustrate a few of the many important contributions that have been made by human service research. Many significant changes will be made in the future as research adds to our knowledge.

WHAT IS RESEARCH?

Every specialized endeavor is characterized by a particular view of the world and a specialized vocabulary. Because human service research is based on methodologies developed for research in the social sciences, and because these methodologies use language in new and unfamiliar ways, human service workers are sometimes bewildered by the world of research.

The purpose of Chapters 1 and 2 is to help you understand the assumptions and worldview that form the basis for social science research, to appreciate the value of research for human service professionals, and to familiarize you with some special vocabulary that we will be using throughout the rest of the book. Once you understand these, human service research will seem less bewildering.

Research can be defined as "a systematic way of asking questions, a systematic method of inquiry" (Drew, 1980, p.4). Research involves a quest for knowledge, one that is conducted in a rational way using scientific methodologies. Its purpose is to discover answers to questions and to accumulate dependable knowledge. Thus human service research is a method for gaining new knowledge about the world.

WHY DO RESEARCH?

Although there are many reasons for doing research, the primary one is that there is a need to further the knowledge of the profession. Thus if research were never done, the human service professions would be based merely on guesswork and speculation. Research must be continually conducted to provide answers to complex questions related to understanding human behavior and establishing effective human service programs and practices.

Many students and professionals in the human services are reluctant to engage in research. They are apprehensive about research courses that they feel are far removed from the real world. Research seems dull compared to the exciting practice of their profession. They believe that their practice skills are sufficient to intervene successfully with individuals, groups, families, organizations, and communities. Despite all of these reservations, knowing about research, either from a consumer's or an investigator's perspective, can be very beneficial to workers in the human services.

Atherton and Klemmack (1982, p. 10) described four important reasons for more involvement in research. Although their arguments are specifically for social workers, their arguments hold true for all human service professionals:

(1) Social workers who are knowledgeable about research would use research techniques for analyzing and processing data, which could lead to better practice and policy decisions.
(2) Social workers who have developed some sophistication in research would be less likely to be deceived by poorly done research.
(3) Social workers with research skills would be in a better position to evaluate the usefulness of research from other disciplines.
(4) Social workers who can participate in research are able to demonstrate accountability to their various constituencies—boards, legislators, and citizens, especially clients.

EARLY BEGINNINGS OF HUMAN SERVICE RESEARCH

In the field of human services some of the earliest pioneers who conducted research were John Howard, Sir Frederic Morton Eden, and Charles Booth (Macdonald, 1960, pp. 6-7). These individuals had a sense of inquiry and became leading advocates for the groups they studied.

John Howard (1726-1790), as a sheriff in Britain, observed that persons who were in prison before their trials and were later acquitted, would often be returned to prison because they had become indebted to their jailer. He devoted considerable effort to studying prisoners, prisons, and jailers and showed the relationship between the judicial system and deplorable conditions that prevailed. Based on his investigations he became a leading social reformer of his time.

Sir Frederic Morton Eden (1766-1809) began his studies by examining the conditions of the poor. Prevailing high prices led him to investigate the impact that these had upon the poor. Later, because of his general interest in pursuing information, he did a history of the Poor Law, and surveyed many parishes to obtain information on wages and living conditions, on industries, on poor-relief practices and workhouse management, and on a variety of related topics. In comparison to modern methods of research, his work had many methodological shortcomings, but he nevertheless obtained important data that had not existed before.

Charles Booth (1840-1916), a wealthy ship owner with a concern about social issues and the poor, undertook a major investigation in London. With the help of his staff, Booth sought to obtain a true picture of life in the city of London. He even lived with a number of poor families in East London in order to have a better understanding of their lives. During 17 years of study he published 17 volumes focusing on poverty, industry, and religion. He has been regarded by many as a great contributor to the early development of social science methodology.

In the United States the origins of human service research can be traced to the early reformers of the 1800s (Macdonald, 1960, pp. 8-9). Although not researchers per se, these reformers gathered data and case histories to bring their cause to the attention of legislators and the general public. Dorothea Dix merits special recognition for her efforts to improve the terrible conditions of the insane, and Jane Addams for her work in the settlement houses. Others, such as Edith and Grace Abbott, Julia Lathrop, and Sophonisba P. Breckinridge studied a variety of social issues, including child welfare, immigration, housing, unemployment, and poverty. These persons were not only social reformers, but they were distinguished scholars as well.

The earliest comprehensive research study conducted in the United States was the Pittsburgh Survey of 1907. This study not only gathered data about the living and working conditions in Pittsburgh, but it also "attempted to identify underlying factors responsible for economic and social conditions" (Macdonald, 1960, p. 9). The study, broad in its scope, examined "industrial conditions (wages, hours, work accidents, and the like); public health, housing, and sanitary conditions; hospitals and other institutions; public education; taxation; crime and criminal justice; playgrounds and recreation; public welfare administration and dependency; even family budgets and home conditions" (Macdonald, 1960, pp. 9-10). The Pittsburgh Survey led to studies in over twenty other cities (Zimbalist, 1977, p. 162), studies that contributed to our understanding of social welfare.

CONCEPTS

Now that you have an understanding of what is meant by research, the value of doing research, and a history of early human service research, let's begin to discuss the vocabulary we will use throughout the rest of this book.

Let's start with the most basic research term: the *concept*. We use concepts all the time. Every word in this book is a concept. What is a concept?

> Definition: A *concept* is a word, term, or symbol that tells us what otherwise different things have in common.

We can illustrate this definition by defining the concept *red*. Now in order to understand this notion of a concept we have to look at the world with a new perspective. So imagine that you are entertaining a visitor from another planet. Your visitor does not have eyes, but rather a technical device that attaches to her head and functions something like a television set. But all the television set devices on your friend's planet are tuned to black and white reception only. Therefore the notion of color is alien to your visitor (so to speak).

Over dinner one evening you notice your visitor pouring catsup into her soup, and someone at the table remarks at how red this year's tomato crop has been. Your visitor looks up, and with a quizzical look on her screen and a tilt of her antennae, says, "Define red."

What's an earthling to do?

Your explanation might sound something like this. "Well, red is something that different objects or ideas have in common. For instance, here is a red pencil, and here is a red crayon. Red is the thing they have in common."

Your friend's screen clears for a moment and she remarks, "I get it, red is something earthlings use to draw."

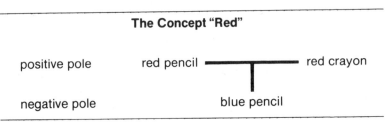

Figure 1.1 Defining the Concept "Red"

Obviously you haven't been clear enough. It turns out that in order to define *red* or any other concept, you must provide not two, but three examples, at a minimum. In order to show that the concept represents something similar in different objects, you must provide at least two examples of things that embody the concept.

You did that when you showed your visitor the red pencil and the red crayon. (These objects are said to form the positive pole of the concept red.) But you also need to show at least one object that is exactly the same as one of the objects you used for the positive pole of the concept, but it must *not* embody the concept. For example, you can show a blue pencil. (This object is said to form the negative pole of the concept *red*.)

The model in Figure 1.1 can be used to define any other concept. For example, how would you define the concept of *aggression*? Your two examples of aggression might be "Jimmy hitting Joey" and "Ms. Grumpy screaming at Mr. Grumpy." Then your example of something that is not aggression might be, "Jimmy sitting quietly reading a novel."

If you think about it, it is difficult to come up with an example of something that is not a concept. That is because our thoughts are formed in terms of words or language, and our language is conceptual. Concepts help us to bring order into the world.

Can you think of something that is not a concept? In order to do that we need a term or symbol that does *not* tell us what otherwise different things have in common. For this, we need to turn to very young children when they are in their preconceptual stage of development and are not yet using language. As an example, the child may know that *chair* refers to the rocker in the living room at home, but he or she doesn't yet understand that the term *chair* also refers to other objects that are used for a similar purpose. So you can see how important concepts are to thinking and hence to research.

Think of the many concepts you use in other settings: age, ethnicity, social welfare program, income, interaction, cognition, services, evaluation, social class, and so on. Try to apply the positive-negative pole definition illustrated in Figure 1.1 to some of these concepts.

> Definition: A *conceptual scheme* is a collection of concepts that are related in some way.

For example, the "systems approach" (Pincus & Minahan, 1973) is a conceptual scheme. It is a way of understanding human service practice by categorizing people into groups such as "change agent system," "client system," and "target system," and categorizing worker relationships into those involving "collaboration," "bargaining," or "conflict." These are, of course, all concepts. Conceptual schemes tie concepts together with assumptions and propositions, such as, "The client system is different from the target system" and "where there are shared goals, influence can be more easily achieved in a collaborative or bargaining relationship than in a conflictual relationship."

Conceptual schemes, when they are well developed through reasoning, logic, or research, can also be called theories. Theories will be discussed in the next chapter.

THE SCIENTIFIC METHOD

We said earlier that human service research, like every specialized endeavor, has a certain view of the world. All social science research is based on the scientific method. This method is a sort of philosophy: It makes certain assumptions and holds certain beliefs about the nature of the world. These assumptions and beliefs can be quite different from our ordinary way of thinking.

The scientific method and our ordinary way of thinking are similar in that they both attempt to order events and explain our world by using concepts and conceptual schemes. But that is where the similarity ends. These two methods can give very different results. For instance, where ordinary thinking leads us to believe that psychiatric patients are violent, if we apply the scientific method we find that psychiatric patients, on the average, are less likely than others to be violent. How do we get two such different conclusions?

Kerlinger (1973) described four ways in which the scientific method differs from what he calls common sense. The first way explains our troubling discrepancy about psychiatric patients. The scientist is *systematic* while the ordinary person is unsystematic. As nonscientists we allow our bias to color our perceptions. If we believe that psychiatric patients are violent, then we tend to take notice whenever we hear of a John Hinckley or a Charles Manson. The media encourage this because they give full coverage to the Hinckleys and Mansons but never mention when a psychiatric patient is *not* violent. That is understandable, but it leads to a wrong conclusion.

The scientist on the other hand, is systematic about the way he or she collects data. Aware that personal biases color our "openness" to new evidence, the scientist will carefully and systematically collect evidence about the relationship between violence and psychiatric status, from all sources. Scientists won't rely on newspaper accounts or personal recollection alone, but will insist on statistics and other consistent sources of information.

This systematic approach will not be limited to collecting evidence. Scientists will also be systematic in the way they build their conceptual schemes and theories, that is, are the underlying propositions clear and consistent? Can the theory be tested in ways that meet acceptable standards of social science research?

The scientists' use of *control* is the second way in which they differ from ordinary persons. Scientists try to understand relationships among events. For instance, as a scientist you may want to understand what factors lead to a serious problem among young people—acne.

Common sense has it that eating chocolate causes acne, and there may be some evidence for this. But as a scientist you don't take this presumed relationship between chocolate and acne at face value! You know that there are many other factors that may lead to acne and that eating chocolate may or may not be one of them. So you use "control." You know that in order to show unequivocally that chocolate leads to acne, you need to rule out all other factors that could possibly lead to development of acne. It may be, for instance, that the highest levels of chocolate consumption occur among young people, and that it is really youth with its flush of hormones that is the culprit in causing acne.

The point is that scientists very carefully look at all the possible events that could cause a particular outcome before they jump to any conclusions. As another example of the idea of control, consider how the scientist determines whether a social service program such as counseling, job training, or child care is effective in making clients happier or more productive. If we find at the end of the program that the client is happier or more productive, we would like to say that this result was due to the program. But before we can do that we have to rule out other possible causes for our success. For example, was it simply the fact that the client got some attention that made the client feel better, and would any program have worked as well? Did our program seem to work because we picked only those clients who were going to improve even without the program? In Chapters 5 and 6 on Research Design we'll show you exactly how these sorts of questions are answered.

The third way in which the scientific method differs from common sense is that the scientist looks for *relationships* among events or factors. It's true that sometimes the scientist is interested only in describing things: Among the clients served by this agency, how many are black and how many white? What is the average age? Or, how many elderly persons on the East Side of town would use the services of a low-cost community health center?

But the real work of the scientist is discovering *relationships* among events or factors: What factors encourage and what factors discourage potential clients from using the services of this agency? What types of health care services are most likely to maintain or improve the health of elderly people?

The fourth characteristic of the scientific method is that the scientist *avoids metaphysical explanations*. A metaphysical explanation is one that cannot be tested. It is usually based on faith, the opinion of others, or "wisdom" passed down through the generations. Examples of metaphysical explanations: "Mary's children are all in trouble with the law because they are 'bad seed.'" "A little suffering is good for the soul." "Mr. Smith didn't survive the accident because his number was called."

The scientist does not claim that such explanations are false, but rather that they fall outside the scope of the scientific method. They are better addressed by religion or other spiritual means. The scientific method is not able to address metaphysical explanations because it is limited to testing only those explanations that have the potential of being shown false. As scientists we never stack the deck in our favor. We set up our explanations and our methods so that we could be shown wrong or right. We also make sure that our evidence is available for anyone to judge. Any other person should be able to look at our evidence and come up with the same conclusion.

So, we do not deal with the explanation that Mary's children are "bad seed." But we might want to test the notion: "Poor economic opportunity and peer relationships with delinquents are likely to lead a teenager into trouble with the law." And we can never say what is "good for the soul."

But we could find out if experiencing pain early in life helps a person to adapt to painful experiences in adulthood.

ARE SCIENTISTS
ALWAYS SCIENTIFIC?

It should be clear that the scientific method is very different from common sense. But do scientists really follow our idealized view of them? Are scientists always scientific?

For the most part they are. But scientists are people too and sometimes they allow their biases, prejudices, sloppiness, or pride to influence their work. Scientists have been known to falsify their results in order to achieve a prized research grant or recognition from their peers. This dishonesty is rare.

A more serious problem is the *distortion* of results that happens when we deviate from the scientific method. This is much more common than outright fraud, and is one of the reasons for you, as a human service worker, to learn about research: to be a critical consumer of research reports so that you can judge the accuracy of the writer's conclusions. Being knowledgeable can also alert you to questions that should have been asked by the researcher but that were not, or data that should have been collected or presented, but were not.

What are some ways in which scientists can violate the scientific method? First, they can be so attached to a preferred view (perhaps because they have spent years defending it and building their career on it) that they ignore or discount evidence that contradicts their view. They can even become illogical or devise elaborate explanations to discount the new evidence so that their preferred view is defended. For example, one of Sigmund Freud's pet theories held that certain effects in his patients were due to seduction by an adult during childhood. When evidence became available that these seductions had not occurred, Freud argued that his patients had imagined these events, and that their *belief* in them caused the same effects (Freud, 1920). He clung to his theory even in the face of contradictory evidence.

Second, scientists can distort the way the research is done or how the data are collected or presented in order to support their personal view. Since scientists are often more passionate than objective in their work, these distortions can work in subtle ways.

An example of the way in which personal views can influence

outcomes is provided by Rosenthal and Jacobson (1968). The researchers randomly selected a number of children in an elementary classroom. Although the children had been randomly selected, their teachers were told instead, that on the basis of extensive testing, these children showed unusual promise for outstanding academic achievement. Testing at the end of the school year showed that these children did actually achieve at higher levels than their classroom peers. The power of suggestion on the teachers was so strong that they actually influenced the results. Their beliefs turned these children from average into high achievers.

Another example of the effect of scientist bias is illustrated by a study of male homosexuals. Bieber (1965) held to the traditional psychoanalytic view that homosexuals are emotionally disturbed and have disturbed family relationships. Not surprisingly, their study of homosexuals confirmed this view. Their subjects had many emotional problems and were likely to have a pathological mother who was described as "close-binding intimate," an undesirable factor according to the researchers.

Other researchers criticized Bieber for being biased. They pointed out that all of Bieber's subjects were men who had entered therapy, a group that was likely to have emotional problems regardless of their sexual orientation. In addition, the interview data were judged by individuals who supported the psychoanalytic-pathology view of homosexuality, so it was not surprising that they found pathology. These researchers had violated the major feature of the scientific method that we mentioned above: Their method did not allow for the possibility that their view could be shown to be incorrect.

A third way in which the scientist is sometimes unscientific is the way in which some scientists fail to open their data to public inspection by other scientists. Some of this is due to the way in which scientific knowledge is usually shared: in professional journals. Journals do not generally publish negative results (i.e., results in which the researcher's contentions were not supported), and therefore much valuable knowledge about what didn't work never sees the light of public scrutiny. Some of it is due to the unwillingness of researchers to present *all* their data. For instance, if four out of five graphs confirm the researcher's contentions, it is all too easy to decide that the fifth graph was unrepresentative, and to leave it out. It is not uncommon for individuals whose scores differed greatly from the norm to be dropped from the analysis.

In addition, researchers may be secretive about data that could be used for the personal gain of competing colleagues. They may want to squeeze that last article out of their data set before making it available to others, or they may want to guard against their competitors using the data to offer competing explanations. The senior author of this book and his colleague were severely criticized some years ago when he used a prominent researcher's data to present a new interpretation of the researcher's well-known study (Berger & Piliavin, 1976a, 1976b).

A fourth and final way in which scientists may be unscientific is the way in which they may rush to support a hypothesis or create a theory, in the absence of supporting data. This is especially true in the human services where a number of intervention models have been popularized with little support from research (Berger, 1986). Simon (1970), commenting on the nature of social casework, noted that casework is very rich in theory (abstract models) but poor in technology (procedures validated by research). Validating procedures by research is a long and painstaking process. Creating a theory is more fun, less work, and, if successful, manages to grab a lot of attention that is often not forthcoming to the meticulous researcher.

WHAT THE SCIENTIFIC METHOD IS AND ISN'T

We've said that the scientific method is characterized by being systematic, using control, looking for relationships among variables, and setting up propositions so that they can be tested objectively. And we've seen that there are many pitfalls on the road to being a truly scientific researcher.

Many people have misunderstandings about science, so it is also important to understand what the scientific method is not (McCain & Segal, 1969).

It is often believed that scientists are concerned mostly with practical questions that affect our day-to-day lives. In this age of high technology it is no wonder that when people think of scientists they think of engineers and other technicians who create bridges, computers, and other useful devices. It is true that these *applied* sciences are vital. But much, perhaps most, of science is *basic* rather than applied, that is, it focuses on the discovery of new knowledge that has no immediate application in the real world.

Most research in the human services is applied. This is due to the nature of our field, which is oriented to meeting real human needs. But it is important to remember that basic science is as important as applied science, and often has long-term real world applications that may not be immediately apparent. Sometimes these applications take many years. In the physical sciences, for instance, Einstein's discovery of the relationship between energy and matter ($E = mc^2$) eventually led to the development of nuclear power. This development could not have been foreseen at the time of Einstein's discovery.

In the same way, Ivan Pavlov, in his work with the salivary response of dogs in the earlier part of this century, established laws of human behavior that today are considered basic. It is not likely that he foresaw the development of psychological techniques that are widely used today to treat anxiety. But these psychological techniques would not have been possible without Pavlov's basic research into behavior.

Another common misunderstanding is that the primary goal of science is collecting facts and information about the world. But, as we saw above, although scientists do collect data, the primary purpose of science is to increase knowledge of how our world operates. This is done by discovering how various events and factors affect each other, and by creating theories to explain and predict. Without theories and propositions to explain why the data are the way they are, the information we collect would be of little use.

Yet another misunderstanding about science is the belief that science is exact. While some believe that this is true only of the physical but not the social sciences, in fact it is true of neither. All scientific propositions are probability statements. For instance, in descriptions of the atom, the exact location of electrons can never be determined; we can state only the probability that an electron will be in a given place at a given time. In the same way, we know that the incidence of infant mortality among lower-class black mothers is higher than among other groups. We can even specify how much higher that probability is. But we cannot predict exactly which mothers will lose their infants. We can only make probability statements about groups of people.

Finally, it is often said that science distorts reality, that it gives a very incomplete picture or understanding of the world. This is perhaps true. Early theories of human behavior such as psychoanalysis and ego psychology provided a very broad understanding of human behavior. Such theories were in fact used to explain a wide variety of phenomenon from personal motivation to humor to politics. But these theories were not scientific.

It is in the nature of scientific theory that it encapsulates and focuses on a very small aspect of the world. In doing so, it predicts and explains, but it may fail to capture the essence of the world as we know it. For example, the germ theory of disease was very effective in explaining and controlling one limited type of health problem (infectious disease) but it told us very little about why and how people stay healthy. Given our current state of knowledge, we have to settle for highly specific but limited theories that explain only small portions of the world, but do so well.

SUMMARY

Human service research is a method of gaining new knowledge about the world. Research has made a significant contribution in addressing a variety of human needs and has great value for the human service practitioner. The origins of human service research date back to the 1700s and 1800s in Great Britain, and in the United States to the early social reformers of the 1800s.

Research, like other specialized endeavors, has a special vocabulary. A concept is a word, term, or symbol that tells us what otherwise different things have in common. The scientific method, like common sense, uses concepts, but is also characterized by systematic inquiry, use of control, the search for relationships among factors, and the avoidance of metaphysical explanations.

Since scientists are human beings they are sometimes unscientific in their work. Good scientific practice is possible when we are open to new interpretations, present our data as completely and objectively as possible, open our work to public scrutiny, and form conclusions based on ample evidence.

Much of science is devoted to generating new knowledge that may not have immediate real world applications. The goal of science is to generate principles that will help us to understand the world. Scientific statements generally focus on events that are limited and specifically defined, and are usually stated in terms of probabilities rather than certainties.

Chapter 2

RESEARCH VOCABULARY

As we mentioned in the last chapter, every specialized endeavor uses a special vocabulary. Human service research is no different, and so in order to understand the material in later chapters of this book we need to define a number of terms. We can think of these terms as building blocks. In this chapter we will define these terms: variable, theory, problem statement, hypothesis, operational definition, independent and dependent variable, and experimental and nonexperimental research.

WHAT IS A VARIABLE?

In Chapter 1 we learned about concepts. Variables are a special type of concept. As Figure 2.1 shows, not all concepts are variables, but all variables are concepts.

> Definition: A *variable* is a concept that varies. It can take on two or more values.

For example, among college students the variable "class standing" can take on the values "freshman," "sophomore," "junior," and "senior." The variable "family income" can take on the values "low," "medium," and "high," or, if we want to be more precise, it can take on any dollar value. It can have literally thousands of different values.

So, in order for a concept to be a variable we must be able to classify it

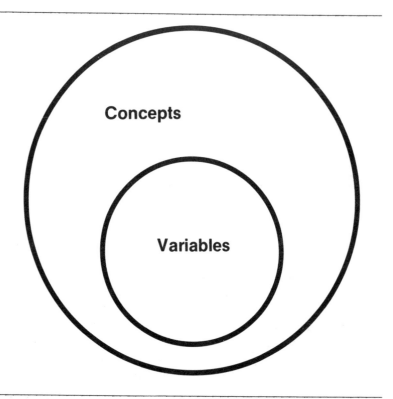

Figure 2.1 Relationship Between Concepts and Variables

into different categories such as low, medium, and high. In order for the concept to be a variable these categories must also meet two criteria: the categories must be *exhaustive* and *mutually exclusive*.

> Definition: A *variable* is a concept that may be classified into two or more exhaustive and mutually exclusive categories.

In order to understand what we mean by saying that categories are exhaustive and mutually exclusive, we need to play a game of marbles. Imagine that we have a bowl of marbles of various colors such as red, green, yellow, and blue. Tomorrow is the big marble swap down at the playground, and in preparation for trading we need to sort our marbles into piles, each pile representing a different color. If we are able to create a pile for each color represented in our marble collection, then we should be able to find a pile for every one of our marbles. If at the end of our sorting, we find that every single marble has been taken out of the bowl and put in its correct color pile, we can say we have exhausted our marbles. (If any marble had been left over, say if we found a chartreuse marble and didn't have a pile or color category to put it into, then our system would not be exhaustive).

> Definition: Categories are *exhaustive* if every object can be placed in a category.

In order for a variable to be a concept its categories or values must not only be exhaustive; they must be mutually exclusive as well. Imagine that in the process of sorting our bowl of marbles we come across a "swirly," a marble that is a mix of different colors. If all our piles or categories are single color, we won't be sure where to put our swirly. Does it belong in the blue pile, the green pile, the yellow pile, or in all of them?

We can't physically place a marble in more than one pile, and we don't want to double count marbles anyway, because at the end we would like to get a count of how many marbles we have of each color. What we want is a way of categorizing marbles that allows each marble to be put into one and only one category.

> Definition: Categories are *mutually exclusive* if each object can be placed in one and only one category.

How do we solve the problem of the swirly marble? The easiest way is probably to create a pile called "mixed colors," or perhaps we could call it simply, "other." Then it would be clear where each marble in our collection belonged. Our categories would then be both exhaustive and mutually exclusive.

When researchers create variables for their studies they play a game similar to our marble game. For example, in a study of the effects of income maintenance programs on different racial groups, we face the task of measuring color ... not the color of marbles but the color of our subjects or clients. Consider the following item on a questionnaire:

PLEASE INDICATE YOUR RACE
BY CHECKING THE APPROPRIATE CATEGORY:

- ____ Caucasian (White)
- ____ Black
- ____ Native American
- ____ Oriental

"Race" is the variable being measured here. But is this really a variable: Are the categories both exhaustive and mutually exclusive? Not really. If I can show that at least one person in my study is not included in these categories, then they are not exhaustive. A person of East Asian descent who does not consider himself or herself a member of the above groups would be such a person. And if I can show that at least one person could be included in more than one group, then the categories are not mutually exclusive. This might be someone of mixed race.

There is no simple solution to the problem of wording the question in such a way that the categories are exhaustive and mutually exclusive, that is, so that the concept of "race" is truly a variable. The solution is to try to figure out all the possibilities that are likely to occur in the persons to be studied. Sometimes you can look at census data or earlier research among your group, to get some idea of its demographic profile, that is, the composition of the group in terms of variables such as race, age, income, and so on.

It will also be important to use wording that is as specific and detailed as possible, to give examples for each category, and to include an "Other" category for someone who might not fit. As long as only a few people check the "Other" category, you can use it without sacrificing too much information about the racial makeup of your group. The following is an example of how one researcher defined the variable "race."

PLEASE CHECK THE ONE CATEGORY
THAT DESCRIBES YOUR RACIAL IDENTITY:

(a) ____ Asian (includes Japanese, Chinese, Korean, and Filipino descent)

(b) ____ Black, non-Hispanic (Includes Afro-American, Jamaican, Trinidadian, West Indian, and African descent)

(c) ____ Hispanic (includes Mexican, Puerto Rican, Cuban, Latin American, or Spanish descent regardless of race)

(d) ____ Indian, American

(e) ____ White, Non-Hispanic

(f) ____ Other (Includes others not covered above and should include Pakistani and East Indian descent, Aleut, Eskimo, Malayan, Thai, and Vietnamese)

It is important to remember that variables *vary*. If a concept cannot take on at least two values it is not a variable. For instance, the following

Values	Variables
family	type of social organization type of dispute type of film
urban	type of residence type of lifestyle
bright	level of intelligence level of achievement
young	(number of years of) age
poor	status of health quality of performance level of achievement

Figure 2.2 Illustration of Values and Variables

concepts are not variables: "family," "bureaucracy," "urban," and "young." Presumably these concepts do not vary, and in fact they might actually represent *values* of variables. "Family" might be one value of the variable "type of social organization," with other values being "friendship network," "social club," "church group," and so on. "Urban" might be one value of the variable "type of residence," with the other values being "rural" and "suburban." Figure 2.2 summarizes several values and associated variables.

Notice that the variables in Figure 2.2 have prefixes that indicate that these are concepts that vary: "type of," "level of," and so on. Variables are not always stated with such prefixes, but they are implied. For instance, when researchers use the variable "age" they really mean "level of age" or "number of years"; when they use the variable "race" they mean "type of race." It is good to keep this in mind. When you are first learning to identify variables it might be handy to attach prefixes to them to remind you that they *vary*.

Concepts and variables give us a way to identify aspects of the world that we are interested in studying. They are the building blocks of theories.

WHAT IS A THEORY?

Definition: A *theory* is an explanation.

We observe something in the world around us and come up with an explanation for what we have observed. For example, if we observe that older persons who seem to have the best adjustment are those who have extensive social networks—family and friends—then we might devise a theory that explains why, how, or under what conditions older people become well adjusted. The theory would include an explanation of the ways in which having friends and family helps in adjustment. Perhaps having close ties makes the older person feel more useful, allows for the exchange of services that makes people feel good, and supports the older person in times of need or crisis.

A theory then, is made up of concepts and variables. A successful theory of aging might be made up of concepts and variables such as social network, peer relationship, life satisfaction, self-esteem, and independence. These will then be joined together to explain successful aging. Kerlinger (1973) provides a more complete definition of a theory.

> Definition: "A theory is a set of inter-related concepts, definitions, and propositions that presents a systematic view of phenomena by specifying relations among variables, with the purpose of explaining and predicting phenomena."

Ideally, a theory will both predict phenomena and also explain why they occur. However, some researchers feel that prediction is sufficient. For example, basic reinforcement theory (also called operant theory) is very useful because it predicts responses even though it doesn't explain *why* they occur. Reinforcement theory tells us, for example, that when Johnny's hand-raising in class is reinforced by attention from the teacher, that response will tend to be repeated. This is useful because it gives us some control over Johnny's behavior: If we want him to raise his hand in class we can increase that response by reinforcing it, that is, following it with teacher attention. If we want to extinguish Johnny's hand-raising we can do so by not following it with reinforcement, that is, by ignoring it.

But notice that reinforcement theory does not explain *why* reinforcement increases Johnny's response. Researchers who were not satisfied with the poor *explanatory* power of reinforcement theory came up with an alternative theory that not only predicts, but also explains why reinforcement leads to an increase in responding. Drive-reduction theory explains that when a response is rewarded some basic drive is reduced. For example, laboratory rats who are reinforced with a drink of water for bar-pressing are likely to increase their bar-pressing because that response results in a reduction of a physiological drive: thirst. In the

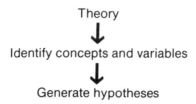

Figure 2.3   Steps in the Research Process

same way, teacher attention may be reinforcing for Johnny because it satisfies a desire for recognition or accomplishment.

Theories that not only predict but also explain why events occur are more satisfying than theories that only predict. Ultimately our curiosity leads us to want to understand not only *what*, but also *how*. Nevertheless, both types of theory are useful in human service research.

It is often said that researchers devise theories and then test them. In a sense that is true. But since theories are made up of abstract concepts and variables, and since it is impossible to measure abstractions, theories are never tested directly. In addition, theories tend to explain a number of different phenomena and we can generally test only one or a few specific phenomena at a time.

In effect, the researcher uses theory to generate specific guesses about how variables are related to one another. Rather than test the theory directly, he or she tests these guesses, which are called hypotheses. To the extent that these hypotheses are confirmed, the researcher can say that the theory is valid.

Figure 2.3 summarizes the steps of the research process that we have discussed so far.

WHAT IS A HYPOTHESIS
AND HOW IS IT TESTED?

Definition: A *hypothesis* is a guess about the nature of the relationship between two or more variables.

For every hypothesis you must be able to identify clearly two or more variables. The hypothesis should also make clear how the researcher believes the variables are related to one another.

Consider the following hypothesis: "Individuals from lower social

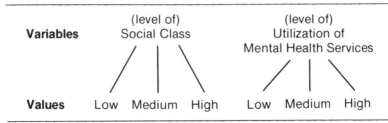

Figure 2.4   Illustration of Two Variables in a Hypothesis

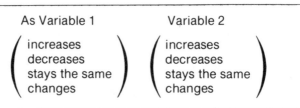

Figure 2.5   A Handy-Dandy Recipe for Writing and Analyzing Hypotheses

classes are less likely to use mental health services, than those from higher social classes."

Can you identify the two variables in this hypothesis? Figure 2.4 lists these variables and their possible values.

Writing hypotheses and identifying the variables in hypotheses that are presented to you are skills just like any others. It takes time to feel comfortable with these new skills. Until you do, you should rely on the handy-dandy recipe in Figure 2.5, which can be used both for writing your own hypotheses and for identifying the variables in others' hypotheses. When you are more comfortable with this skill you can throw away the recipe, just like you threw away those trainer wheels when you first learned how to ride a bicycle.

If we apply this recipe to the hypothesis above we should get something like this: "As social class decreases, the utilization of mental health services decreases." This makes it easy to identify the two variables in the hypothesis.

Here are some additional hypotheses. Can you identify the variables in each of them?

- As the size of workers' caseloads increases, client satisfaction with agency services decreases.

- As availability of day care services increases, the proportion of mothers who work outside the home increases.
- Poorly assimilated ethnic groups are less likely to utilize services than well assimilated ethnic groups.
- Older persons with few leisure interests will have greater difficulty adjusting to retirement than older persons with many leisure interests.
- Clients in short-term treatment show greater clinical improvement than clients in long-term treatment.

A well-constructed hypothesis will meet two criteria.

(1) It will clearly state the relationship between two or more variables.
(2) It will use variables that can potentially be measured. (For instance, in our first hypothesis there are ways to measure individuals' social class and mental health.)

There will of course be times when our handy-dandy recipe for hypotheses will not be up to snuff . . . just like those training wheels can hold you back from a very fast bike race. One example is when the relationship between variables is more complex. What, for example, if utilization of mental health services decreases as social class decreases for those in the middle classes? But for those of very low social class, utilization might actually increase because of a higher utilization of public institutions. Under these circumstances the hypothesis should state: "As social class decreases, utilization of mental health services initially decreases and then increases as social class falls below the middle-class level."

What about hypotheses that state the relationship among more than two variables? Three variable hypotheses can be helpful in giving us a better picture of how groups of variables affect one another. For example, a local community mental health center may find when they study all their clients, that utilization of services do in fact decrease consistently as the social class of those in its service area decreases.

But a knowledgeable agency staff member may suggest a more detailed hypothesis: "For those under 65 years of age, as social class decreases, utilization decreases. For those 65 and older there is no difference in utilization as social class changes." In order for the agency to test this refined hypothesis they will have to look at the relationship between social class and utilization twice: once for those under 65, and again for those 65 and older. To the two original variables in our hypothesis (social class and utilization of services) we have added a third variable (age).

Here is another example of a three-variable hypothesis: "For elementary school children, tangible rewards are more effective than praise in increasing academic performance, while for high school children praise is more effective."

Can you identify the three variables? (They are type of reward, level of academic performance, and grade level).

Are four, five, and more variable hypotheses possible? Yes, but they are not desirable because they are difficult to understand and therefore cause confusion. There are of course many situations in which we want to know how several variables affect each other. And there are statistical techniques suited to such analyses.

For example, a well-known study found that frail elderly clients who received casework services died sooner than those who were not served (Blenkner, Bloom, & Nielsen, 1971). In an attempt to figure out the reasons for this disturbing result, the senior author and his colleague looked at the simultaneous effect of a number of variables operating together and their impact on survival of clients. These variables included the older person's age, mental status, and physical abilities (Berger & Piliavin, 1976a, 1976b). In situations such as this, which involve groups of variables, it is best to simplify: State your hunches as a *series* of two- or three-variable hypotheses.

As we have seen, hypotheses can be classified into two-variable and three-variable hypotheses. There is one other way in which hypotheses are classified, and that is according to the nature of the relationship that is stated. There are three possibilities.

(1) The hypothesis states that there is no relationship between variables (as one changes the other one stays the same) or that there is no difference between groups (say, between those who received services and those who did not). This is called the *null hypothesis*.

(2) The hypothesis states that there is a relationship between variables or a difference between groups. There are two possibilities in this instance:
   (a) The hypothesis states the direction of the relationship or difference, for example, "Human service students are more intelligent than business students" or "Human service students are less intelligent (sorry!) than business students." This is called a *directional* hypothesis.
   (b) The hypothesis does not state the direction of the relationship or it does not say how the groups will differ (which one will be better), for

example, "Human service students differ from business students in level of intelligence." This is called a *nondirectional* hypothesis.

These distinctions among hypotheses are important because they have implications for how we analyze our data. This is discussed further in Chapter 5 of *Implementing the Research Plan* (Sage Human Services Guide 51), in the section entitled "Statistical Hypothesis Testing."

DESCRIPTIVE RESEARCH

As we have said, the scientist studies relationships among variables and this is done by testing hypotheses derived from theories. Most human service research follows this pattern.

However, there is an important type of research called descriptive research, which does not use hypotheses. In some instances, rather than studying relationships among variables, we are simply interested in describing a group of persons, families, organizations, or communities. We describe each of these entities one variable at a time.

For example, if I am interested in studying the human service needs of an underserved neighborhood I might want to begin by doing a survey to get a description of the types of people who live in that neighborhood: What is the age distribution? How many live in families and how many live alone? What sort of incomes do people have? In my survey I might ask some questions to find out what services if any, are needed: What medical facilities do you use? Is day care available to you? What do you do for recreation? What services would you use if they were available?

When is descriptive research used? It is used anytime we are interested in describing an individual, group, organization, or community. Descriptive research is used, for example, when we are assessing needs, such as the need for a day care center in a neighborhood. It is often used when we have no theory to work from, or when we are beginning to explore a new area that has not been researched before. In this case there is no body of knowledge to guide us in formulating hypotheses. The purpose of our research then may be simply to describe a phenomenon so that we will be better able to study it in the future. Our descriptive research will help us to understand better what we are studying so that we may later be able to create theories and hypotheses for future research.

Despite the importance of descriptive research, our research efforts are most worthwhile when we work from theories and hypotheses. We make guesses about how variables are related to one another, and we study these relationships. This is done by testing hypotheses. Since hypotheses are made up of variables, we will need some way of measuring variables in order to test our hypotheses. And in order to measure our variables we need to *define* them *operationally*.

OPERATIONAL DEFINITIONS

Definition: An *operational definition* tells us what activities or operations we need to perform in order to measure a concept or variable.

Assume our hypothesis is "As the level of income increases, the utilization of psychotherapy increases." In order to test this hypothesis we will need some way of measuring each of its variables: level of income and (level of) utilization of psychotherapy.

The operational definition for level of income might be "gross income as reported on line 32 of the individual's latest federal income tax form."

The operational definition for utilization of psychotherapy might be "the individual's response to the interview question: 'Within the past six months how many hours of service did you receive from a psychotherapist? Indicate the number of hours such as 0 for no visits, 3 for three hours of service, and so on.'"

Creating operational definitions for your concepts and variables allows you to be creative because there is usually no one correct way to define them operationally. Can you detect possible flaws or alternatives to the operational definitions above? For homemakers a better approximation of income might be line 32 of their spouse's tax form. If it is available, should income reported on a joint return be used as the best operational definition? What if the couple filed a joint return but are currently separated? These are the sorts of issues you will need to handle in coming up with the best operational definitions for your concepts and variables.

At first it is difficult to think in terms of operational definitions because they are very different from the kinds of definitions we are used to. Operational definitions are different from dictionary definitions. Consider the dictionary definition of the variable we operationally defined above: income. According to the dictionary, *income* is "the money or other gain periodically received by an individual, corporation, etc., for labor or services, or from property, investments, operations, etc." (*Webster's New World Dictionary*, 1964).

The dictionary definition for *psychotherapy* is "the application of various forms of mental treatment, as hypnosis, suggestion, psychoanalysis, etc., to nervous and mental disorders" (*Webster's New World Dictionary*, 1964). This definition does not tell us what steps we must take to identify the concept *psychotherapy*. An operational definition of psychotherapy might be, "Professional services rendered by any individual currently listed in the Registry of Clinical Psychologists, the Academy of Certified Social Workers or licensed as a clinical psychologist, social worker or marriage and family counselor in this state." This operational definition is useful to researchers because it specifies what they must do in order to measure the concept, that is, they must find the individual on one of the relevant lists. Any such individual is to be considered a psychotherapist.

Dictionary definitions are useful in helping us to understand what concepts mean. They generally provide synonyms or examples of the concept. But they are useless for research because they fail to tell us how to measure our concepts and variables.

Operational definitions are also different from attribute definitions. Attribute definitions define concepts by specifying what they consist of. For instance, an attribute definition of *apple pie* might be "a dessert prepared from flour, water, yeast, apples, and sugar." But if I actually wanted to make an apple pie, an operational definition would be more useful: "an apple pie is a food item prepared according to the recipe for 'apple pie' that appears on page 56 of the *American Desserts Cookbook*."

As we've said, there is some creativity in coming up with good operational definitions. But what makes for a good operational definition? There are two criteria that should be met.

First, the operational definition should be *reliable or replicable*. Good operational definitions are so clearly stated that two independent researchers, following the same operational definition, will measure the same concept or variable in exactly the same way. For example, if I define *income* as an individual's gross income as reported in their latest federal tax return, there should be no trouble in coming up with a consistent figure even if I send different researchers to collect the information. If my instructions are clear enough, anyone should be able to come up with the same figure.

Second, the operational definition should be *valid*. Validity is more difficult to achieve than reliability. An operational definition is valid to the extent that it measures the variable or concept in such a way that it reflects its "true" meaning.

It is possible for an operational definition to be reliable but not valid. Suppose, for example, that a rather naive anthropologist from another culture decided that he or she would identify Americans who are "in love" by observing whether or not they held hands with another person. With a little work we could probably come up with a reliable definition of *holding hands* that would be consistent enough so that it could be used with the same results by independent observers strategically placed in city parks on warm summer afternoons. That is, our observers would agree most of the time on which individuals fell into the two categories of "holding hands" and "not holding hands."

But we would question the validity of this operational definition as a measure of being "in love." Holding hands may be a reliable, but it is not a valid, definition of being "in love," because many people who hold hands are not in love and vice versa.

A more realistic example of an operational definition, which is reliable but possibly not valid, concerns the use of standardized intelligence tests with cultural and racial minorities. Tests such as the Wechsler Adult Intelligence Scale are reliable: They will result in the same or similar IQ scores when repeatedly used on the same individuals and they are consistent over time as well. But critics of these tests argue that they are culture-bound. For individuals who are not familiar with white middle-class terms and concepts these tests may not be *valid* measures of native intelligence (Bourne & Ekstrand, 1982, pp. 201-210).

In order to avoid confusion later it is useful to point out that *reliability* and *validity* are characteristics that are applied to at least three different aspects of research methods. We have just discussed the reliability and validity of operational definitions. Two separate issues that we will discuss in later chapters are the reliability and validity of research designs (in this volume), and the reliability and validity of measuring instruments such as questionnaires and interview schedules (in *Implementing the Research Plan*).

So far we have learned about theories, concepts, variables, hypotheses, and operational definitions. Figure 2.3 illustrated that research proceeds according to a certain order: theory comes first. Concepts and variables are then used to construct hypotheses derived from theory. The remaining steps are shown in Figure 2.6. The concepts and variables in the hypotheses are operationally defined. In telling you how to measure these concepts and variables, operational definitions allow you

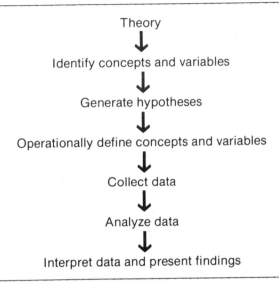

Figure 2.6   Steps in the Research Process

to collect data, which are later analyzed, and interpreted. *Implementing the Research Plan* will discuss data collection, analysis and interpretation, and the presentation of results.

Interpretation of data and presentation of results is never the final step in the research process. Our findings continually lead us to modify, expand, or even abandon our theories, so when the steps in Figure 2.6 have been completed we can think of them recycling over and over again.

There is, however, one caution that we must observe. When we use our data to modify or create theory, we must confirm that theory with an *independent* set of data. In other words, we should not use data to create a theory and then use those same data to argue that our theory is correct. Why not?

If we use the same data to create a theory *and* to confirm it, we have violated one of the rules of the scientific method that we discussed in Chapter 1. When we use the same data to both create a theory and confirm it, we are stacking the deck in our favor: We are creating a situation in which our propositions cannot be shown to be false. That does not mean that we should not look to our results to modify or create theory. We *should* do that. But in order to confirm that modification or that new theory, we need to use an independently collected set of data.

EXPERIMENTAL AND
NONEXPERIMENTAL RESEARCH

We have now defined most of the concepts we will need in order to get into the "meat" of research: stating research questions and getting answers to them. But first we need to establish some additional research vocabulary.

As we said earlier, the scientist looks for relationships between and among variables. In this process we usually need to distinguish between two types of variables.

> Definition: In a two-variable relationship the *independent variable* is the one that comes first. The *dependent variable* comes second.

We can think of the independent variable as the presumed "cause" and the dependent variable as the presumed "effect." (Note that we use the word *presumed*. Just because two variables are related does not mean that one "causes" the other.)

For example, when we evaluate the effect of human service programs on clients, participation in the program is generally the independent variable and the intended change in the client is the dependent variable. Consider the hypothesis: "Participation of preschool children in the Head Start Program enhances their academic performance in grade school." Participation in Head Start is the independent variable because it comes first. Level of academic performance in grade school comes later: It is the dependent variable.

Demographic variables such as race, age, occupational status, and social class are generally independent variables. Typically we look at the effects of these independent variables on outcomes, or dependent variables. For example, we might be interested in studying the impact of race (independent variable) on attitudes toward the use of birth control by teenagers (dependent variable).

However, the situation is not always clear cut. There are situations in which it is difficult to tell which is the independent and which the dependent variable. For example, it has been known that the incidence of severe mental illness is higher among the lower socioeconomic classes. For a long time it was assumed that socioeconomic status was the independent variable. That is, researchers believed that lower class status, with its economic deprivation and lack of resources, led to stress that in turn led to a higher incidence of mental illness.

But it may be the other way around: Mental illness may lead to low socioeconomic status. That is, the mental illness may prevent the person from functioning in social and occupational roles, and that may cause the person to remain in or drop to a lower socioeconomic class. In this view, mental illness is the independent variable.

There are plenty of examples of situations in which it is difficult or impossible to identify the independent and dependent variables. We know that intelligent people tend also to be creative. But which one came first? It is also true that people who like each other tend to have similar interests. But do they like each other because they have similar interests, or have they developed similar interests because they like each other? One of the functions of theory is to explain such relationships so that we can understand which are the independent and which are the dependent variables.

Is it always important to distinguish between independent and dependent variables? When you are studying relationships among variables, it *is* important. Differentiating among variables helps us to better understand how they are related and it determines the way we present our data and interpret our results. This will become more clear after you have studied the rest of this book.

Differentiating between independent and dependent variables also helps us to distinguish between two types of research that we will be studying in more detail in Chapter 5. They are defined here.

Definition: *Experimental* research is research in which the independent variable is manipulated by the researcher. In *nonexperimental* research the researcher has no control over the independent variable.

One type of experimental research is often used to evaluate the effectiveness of human service programs. In this type of study the researcher assigns some individuals to participate in a program, while another group of individuals does not. The researcher can then compare the two groups to see if the program worked. This is a case of experimental research because the researcher manipulated the independent variable of "participation in the program," that is, the researcher determined who was going to participate and who was not going to participate in the program. So, when the researcher controls who will receive the different levels of the independent variable (in this case, participation versus no participation in the program), then we say that the researcher manipulated the independent variable. This means that the research was experimental.

In many situations the researcher cannot manipulate the independent variable, that is, the researcher cannot determine who will be in one group or the other. Let's say, for example, that the researcher wanted to study the level of job satisfaction among different types of human service workers. He or she may hypothesize that those who work in public welfare agencies are less satisfied with their jobs than those who work for private agencies. The independent variable here is "type of agency" and its values are "public welfare agency" and "private agency."

Since the researcher does not have the power to assign some workers to work in public agencies and others to work in private agencies, all the researcher can do is locate workers in the two types of agencies and ask them about their job satisfaction. In other words, it wasn't the researcher who manipulated the independent variable. It was already "manipulated" by nature, circumstance, or fate, and the researcher merely came onto the scene after the fact. Therefore this type of study is nonexperimental.

Although it is often desirable for the researcher to manipulate the independent variable (we'll learn why in Chapter 5), in most situations in the human services this is just not possible. Here are some examples of research hypotheses that would be studied using nonexperimental research. See if you can identify the independent and dependent variables and explain why these questions would have to be studied using nonexperimental research.

(a) Older persons have more positive attitudes about aging than do younger persons.
(b) Human service students are more altruistic than business administration students.
(c) Families with a developmentally disabled child are more likely than other families to be involved in community activities.
(d) As level of family income increases, willingness to contribute to the United Way increases.

In the case of each of the above hypotheses, the researcher is not able to manipulate the independent variable. Therefore each hypothesis would have to be tested using a nonexperimental study.

SUMMARY

This chapter completes our understanding of the basic language of human service research. We saw that variables are special types of concepts, and that theories, which serve as explanations, are constructed from concepts, variables, and propositions. In order to see if our theories are valid, we derive hypotheses from them and then test these hypotheses. But first we must operationally define the concepts and variables in our hypotheses. It is also useful to distinguish between independent and dependent variables, and experimental and non-experimental research. Given the tools we have learned in Chapters 1 and 2 we can now go on to defining a researchable problem.

Chapter 3

SEARCHING THE LITERATURE AND DEFINING A RESEARCHABLE PROBLEM

In the previous chapter you learned some new vocabulary related to research. In this chapter we are going to introduce you to the notion of a "research problem" and explain how you can use the literature in doing your research. A research problem is often stated in the form of a question. For example, a research problem might be, "What effect does client resistance have on counseling?" or "Does the provision of case management services keep elderly persons from going into a nursing home?" A research problem can also be written as one or more statements that express the purpose of a study. The following research problems were taken from the literature and are expressed in the form of statements:

> The study analyzed the differences and similarities between DSW and Ph.D. graduates in social work, regarding their educational and demographic characteristics, their reasons for entering the doctoral programs, their academic experiences within the doctoral programs, and their employment patterns before and after receiving the doctorate. (Patchner, 1983a)

> The study was designed to determine the primary sources of stress encountered when students enter alternative graduate programs, assess whether these stresses are different from those who enter traditional programs, and identify the kinds of support services necessary to minimize the stresses they encounter. (Patchner, 1983b)

A research problem specifies the purpose and scope of a study and it helps guide the scientific procedures used to conduct the study. Research problems often indicate whether the study will test for differences between variables or examine the relationship between them. For instance, in the previous examples the first examined similarities and differences among Ph.D.s and DSWs, while the second research problem examined the relationship among variables, namely, the type of student (i.e., those in alternative programs and those in traditional graduate programs) and the sources of stress. Studies that test for differences between variables often use the words *differ* or *difference* in the research problem, while studies that examine relationships often use the words *related to* or *relationship* in the problem statement. Therefore, the researcher must carefully select the words used in specifying the research problem because they affect the meaning of the study and they give an indication of the type of research design and data analysis that will be used.

FORMULATING A
RESEARCHABLE PROBLEM

The process of formulating researchable problems involves a number of steps. The process consists of (1) identifying a general problem area, (2) relating the research problem to existing theory, (3) stating the research problem, (4) defining concepts and variables, (5) developing operational definitions, and (6) examining the relationship among variables or describing phenomena. The process can be conceptually thought of as a funnel or an inverted triangle in which the scope of the study becomes increasingly narrow.

Let's examine how a student doing an internship at a community mental health center can formulate a research problem using this process. The student is interested in studying the concept of client resistance and originally described the research problem as a study of client resistance.

The first step in formulating a research problem is to identify a general subject area for study. In this example the student's idea of studying client resistance is the general subject area. Starting with a general subject helps to provide a beginning focus for the study. Research frequently begins this way with a curiosity about some phenomenon, problem, or theory. The search for knowledge does not always begin with a clearly defined research problem or explicit hypotheses. Often research is undertaken because the investigator is curious about, interested in, or perplexed by something.

After identifying the general problem area, the next step is relating the research problem to existing theory. A study should never be done in a vacuum, but should take place within the body of knowledge that currently exists. Examining how a study is connected to previous knowledge and using this knowledge as a guide can be of great benefit in designing the study, interpreting results, and generalizing the findings to other people. Moreover, it helps practitioners contribute to the knowledge base of their practice or more generally to the knowledge base of their profession. In this example, the student reviewed the literature on client resistance to examine relevant theories about client resistance in counseling and to see what had been found in other research studies.

The next step, stating the research problem, requires narrowing the focus of the study and explicitly knowing its purpose. The researcher must take the general subject area of the study and the knowledge gained from reviewing the literature and then precisely state the research problem. Knowing the research problem gives the investigator a framework from which all other aspects of the study flow. In this example the student specifically formulated the research problem as a question: "What effect does client resistance have on counseling?"

Another important task in formulating research problems is defining concepts and variables. As you learned in Chapter 2, a concept is a word, term, or symbol that tells what otherwise different things have in common, and a variable is a concept that can take on two or more values. Defining concepts and variables in a study is a necessary step to provide further clarity to the research problem. In this example the concept of client resistance is not clear. The student, therefore, defined the concept of client resistance as the degree to which a client fails to follow instructions. In defining client resistance in this manner the study becomes clearer and more focused.

The next step is to define operationally the variables in the study. Operational definitions, as you now know, tell what activities or operations need to be performed in order to measure a concept or variable. In this example, the student had to define client resistance operationally within the conceptual framework of the more general

Broad Concept
Client Resistance

Research Problem
What effect does client resistance have on
counseling?

Defining the Concept
Client resistance further defined as:
    The degree to which a client fails to follow
    instructions.

Operational Definition
Client resistance defined as:
    Client arrives for appointment more than 10
    minutes late.
    Client fails to collect and submit between-
    session data.

Hypotheses
1. Clients with high levels of resistance are more
   likely to drop out of counseling.
2. Clients with high levels of resistance are less
   likely to report a decrease in anxiety.

Figure 3.1 Defining a Research Problem

definition of "a client failing to follow a counselor's instructions." The
student needed to be able to measure what was meant by this. Therefore,
the student operationally defined client resistance as (1) the client
arriving more than 10 minutes late for a scheduled appointment, and (2)
the client failing to collect and submit between-session data. Now the
concept of client resistance can be measured by seeing how often clients
were late and how often they failed to collect data between their
counseling sessions. These operational definitions clear up any ambi-

guity in the meaning of client resistance and they can easily be measured.

Having sufficiently narrowed the focus of the study the student was now able to examine the relationships that existed between the variables. This is usually done by stating hypotheses, or in exploratory-descriptive studies, by asking specific research questions. In this example, the student stated two hypotheses that he or she wanted to test: (1) clients with high levels of resistance are more likely to drop out of counseling, and (2) clients with high levels of resistance are less likely to report a decrease in anxiety.

Some types of research simply seek to describe certain phenomena or groups of people, rather than describing relationships among variables. In this study of client resistance, for instance, the student might have asked, "What are the demographic characteristics (e.g., age, sex, income) of clients who are resistant to treatment?" This type of research is known as descriptive research.

Figure 3.1 illustrates the process of formulating a research problem that we just went through with the student's study on client resistance as an example. Notice how the study became more focused as we went through each of the steps.

Selltiz, Wrightsman, and Cook (1976) specified three criteria for formulating a "researchable problem" (i.e., a problem amenable to being researched). First, the concepts must be clear enough so that one can specify in words exactly what the question is. Second, the concepts must be such that they can be represented by some sort of evidence that is obtainable through direct observation or other less direct activities. Third, it must be feasible to carry out such operations or activities. As you can see, after going through all of the steps in formulating a research problem our example clearly meets these criteria.

SEARCHING THE LITERATURE

A very important step that permeates the development of a researchable problem and is an integral component of the entire research process is reviewing the literature. The literature search enables the investigator to examine relevant theories, previous research, and scholarly inquiry into the area of study. It helps provide a framework for the study and serves the function of (1) discovering findings from previous research on the general problem, (2) finding relevant theories that apply to the investigation being undertaken, and (3) informing the investigator of various methodologies and research procedures to study the problem.

The literature search begins in the library, which contains a wealth of information and is an essential resource in conducting research. There are various types of literature that are available for review and the beginning researcher needs to know the basic differences between these. One type includes primary sources of information such as journal articles, government and technical reports, dissertations, and books that contain original research. These furnish the best information available to the researcher. Another type of literature is secondary sources that are summarized and reevaluated versions of primary literature. The most common forms of secondary literature are textbooks and encyclopedias, such as the *Encyclopedia of Social Work*. Review of these sources is helpful because they provide a synthesis of original works and generally list references so the researcher can refer to the primary sources. Let's now look at the major library resources that can be used to help with the literature search.

LIBRARY RESOURCES

The Card Catalog

The card catalog is a listing of all of the books in the library. It generally provides the following information about the books located in the library.

- title
- author
- date and place of publication
- edition
- publisher
- total number of pages
- call number
- library (i.e., the specific library within the library system where the book is located)

This information is entered on cards that may vary in size and style from one library to another. The cards are filed alphabetically and are cross-referenced by author, title, and subject. Therefore, you could find books by looking in the card catalog under the author's name, the title, or the general subject. For example, if you were doing research on the topic of psychoanalysis, you could look under the subject of psychoanalysis and find books pertaining to this subject, or you could look for the books written by a specific author, such as Sigmund Freud, or if you knew the title of a book, but not the author, you could look under the alphabetical listing of the title. Although the card catalog lists the holdings of books in the library, some holdings such as government documents, reference books, or periodicals may not be referenced. Therefore, you might have to seek the assistance of a librarian to help you to obtain these sources.

The usual way of listing books in the card catalog is rapidly changing. Because of computer technology, many libraries are converting their card catalog to on-line computer files. These systems are not only fast, but they reduce the error of overlooking important works that might be missed by manually going through drawers of file cards in the card catalog. In addition, they provide current information regarding the status of books you have identified as potential sources. For example, you may learn if the book has been checked out or if it on the shelf; and, if the book has been checked out, the computer will tell you when it is due to be returned and will allow you to reserve it. The computerized card catalog is quite easy to use. The library makes computer terminals available that users can easily access. Simple commands are typed by using the keyboard and then the appropriate references appear on the computer screen. The computerized card catalog system at the University of Illinois at Urbana—Champaign works in the following manner:

To search a title the command TLS is typed, followed by a slash and then the first four letters of the first significant word in the title and five letters of the next significant word. For example, if you were interested in books that had titles that started with the words mental health, you would type TLS/menthealt. All books in the library with titles that begin with Mental Health, The mental health, A mental health, and so on would be then listed on the computer screen.

To search for a specific author you would enter the command AUT, followed by a slash and the first six letters of the last name and the first three letters of the first name. For example, to find the works of an author named Raymond Berger you would type AUT/bergerray.

Abstracts and Indexes

Abstracts and indexes are secondary sources of information that summarize and categorize original works. Abstracts provide brief summaries of published articles and list all information necessary to locate the original work. Indexes categorize published works by subject, author, or by some other means. A number of indexes will also provide brief summaries of the works listed. Abstracts and indexes constitute a primary method of finding references on particular topics. Whereas the card catalog serves as the primary source for locating books in a subject area, abstracts and indexes serve as the major sources for locating articles and other periodical literature. The major abstracts and indexes with which researchers in the human services should be familiar include *Social Work Research and Abstracts*, *Sociological Abstracts*, *Psychological Abstracts*, *Current Index to Journals in Education*, and the *Social Science Citation Index*. In addition, if your research is in the area of social welfare policy, you will want to consult the *Monthly Catalog of United States Government Publications*.

Social Work Research and Abstracts, published by the National Association of Social Workers, includes original research articles and also abstracted works published in over 250 professional and academic journals in social work, social welfare, and related fields. Abstracts of recent doctoral dissertations in social work appear in the fall issue.

Sociological Abstracts, published by the American Sociological Association, covers the literature in sociology and other related disciplines in the social and behavioral sciences. It concentrates on the core journals in sociology with selective coverage of journals in other disciplines when the articles pertain to sociology or when they were written by sociologists. It covers approximately 140 sociology and 400 social science journals, including international sources.

Psychological Abstracts, published monthly by the American Psychological Association, selectively abstracts more than 950 journals. It contains summaries of research in the sixteen major areas of psychology. Many of these areas also contain subcategories. Each issue includes a guide that is useful in using and understanding the abstracts.

Current Index to Journals in Education is a comprehensive source published monthly by the Educational Resources Information Center (ERIC). It abstracts articles from over 750 journals in education and related fields.

The *Social Science Citation Index*, published by the Institute for Scientific Information, is an interdisciplinary index to social science literature. It indexes about 4,500 social science journals in all disciplines. It is made up of the *Source Index*, which includes all authors of the articles listed in the year that is covered, the *Citation Index*, which lists authors cited in the articles covered during the year, the *Permuterm Subject Index*, which provides a subject listing, and the *Corporate Author Index*, which references works that do not have a personal author, such as those published by an organization or agency.

The *Monthly Catalog of United States Government Publications* annually includes some 27,000 congressional and departmental documents issued by all branches of the government.

These abstracts and indexes are very valuable resources for the researcher. Many other abstracts and indexes do exist and they may be helpful, depending on the focus of your research and literature search. They are generally more specialized but, with the help of the librarian to direct you to these sources, they could also be consulted. For example, the *Current Literature on Aging* specializes in articles and books in gerontology, the *Human Resources Abstracts* indexes journal articles in the area of employment and unemployment, the *Exceptional Child Resources* will include sources related to handicapped children, and *Criminal Justice Abstracts* will include abstracts of articles in the field of criminal justice, including probation, child abuse, elder abuse, and domestic violence. If you have difficulty in locating or using the appropriate abstracts and indexes, ask your librarian who will show you where they are located in your library and will instruct you in using them.

Journals

Journals are a primary source of information and are referenced in abstracts and indexes. Some journals are specialized while others are more general in their focus. Some are refereed and others are nonrefereed. A refereed journal is one that has an editorial board that reviews each article that is submitted for publication to the journal. A panel of two or three editorial board members reads an article and then decides to publish it as it is, to have the author revise and then publish it, or to reject it for publication. This process usually results in a more objective review of an article by persons who are very knowledgeable about the field. A usual indicator of whether a journal is refereed is to look at the journal and examine if the names of persons serving on the editorial board are listed. If an editorial board is listed, then the journal is most likely refereed; if just an editor is listed, then the journal is probably nonrefereed. Many professional journals are available to social workers and other human service professionals. Some major journals, listed according to selected interest areas, include the following:

Administration and Supervision

Administration in Social Work
Clinical Supervisor

Aging and Gerontology

Activities, Adaptation, and Aging
Clinical Gerontologist
The Gerontologist
Journal of Gerontological Social Work

Child Welfare and Family Services

Child Care Quarterly
Child Welfare
Clinical Social Work Journal
Family Process
Family Relations
Journal of Family Issues
Smith Studies in Social Work

General Social Work and Social Welfare

Arete
Human Services in the Rural Environment
Journal of Sociology and Social Welfare
Public Welfare
Social Service Review
Social Work

Health Care

Health and Social Work
Social Work in Health Care
Home Health Care Services Quarterly

Mental Health

Administration in Mental Health
American Journal of Orthopsychiatry
Community Mental Health Journal
Prevention in Human Services

Methods and Treatment

American Journal of Family Therapy
Case Analysis: In Social Science and Social Therapy
Journal for Specialists in Group Work
Social Casework
Social Work with Groups

Schools

School Social Work Journal
Social Work in Education

Women

Women and Health
Women and Therapy

Computer Searches

As the computerized card catalog assists in locating relevant books, the computer bibliographic search assists in locating relevant journal articles. Most major libraries have access to data bases that are computerized versions of indexes and abstracts. Most of the major abstracts and indexes that are available in print are computerized. However, there are a number of data bases that are computerized, but do not have a counterpart available in print. Librarians, who are trained in computer search procedures, access these data bases by typing a few key words or phrases into a computer terminal. Within minutes the computer is able to generate a listing of all of the citations available on the given topic. If requested, the listing will also include an abstract of each of the articles cited.

The librarian must have accurate information about the focus of the literature search to give the proper commands to the computer. For example, if we were interested in searching the topic of depression, we would have to let the librarian know that we meant psychological depression. Otherwise, we might get references for journal articles related to the Great Depression of the 1930s. Often a number of key words are cross-referenced to narrow the search. For example, if we were interested in the topic of counseling terminally ill cancer patients, the search would produce articles dealing only with this specific topic and not all articles in the data base pertaining to counseling, all of those pertaining to terminal illness, and all pertaining to cancer.

Usually there is a charge for this service that may range from $5 to $30 for each data base utilized. The charges may be well worth the money considering the time saved. However, one should be aware that some relevant articles might be missed because they are not listed in the particular data base being searched and that the computer might list a number of articles that are not directly related to the focus of your research. Therefore, the computerized search should be viewed as having great supplemental value to the literature search process, but it should not replace the browsing and serendipitous discovery that exists with printed abstracts and indexes, as imperfect as they sometimes are.

STEPS IN THE
LITERATURE SEARCH

Without a doubt, the main consideration in doing a relevant literature search is to have a well-defined researchable problem. Understandably, some literature review may have been necessary to get to this point, but without a clear focus of the research, the literature search will have little direction and much time may be spent finding resources that are only marginally useful. Although there is no one precise way of searching the literature, the following steps can serve as a guide to help give a perspective on the process.

(1) Know the focus of the research by having a well-defined research problem.

(2) Select key words relevant to the research topic. These can then be used when going through the card catalog and searching the abstracts and indexes. For example, if a research project focused on counseling terminally ill cancer patients, the key words might include counseling, therapy, terminal illness, death and dying, and cancer patients.

(3) Go to the card catalog and identify books that relate to the topic.

(4) Locate and read the books or appropriate sections of the books. Look for relevant references that were cited in the bibliography of these books and locate the references cited.

(5) Tell the librarian about your topic and ask for assistance in identifying and using the proper abstracts and indexes.

(6) Review appropriate abstracts and indexes (either manually or through a computerized search) to identify articles that are related to the research topic. Locate and read the articles. Be sure to examine the references that are cited.

(7) Know the procedures for interlibrary loan because a number of articles that you identify might be in journals not subscribed to by your library. Therefore, you will have to obtain these sources through interlibrary loan. This process usually takes several weeks and often a charge is required.

(8) Locate and review other relevant documents, such as government reports, statistical information, dissertations, and theses. Ask the librarian for help in locating these materials.

When doing a literature search it is important to remember that until you become familiar with using the card catalog, the indexes and abstracts, and other resources available in the library, perhaps the most important resource in the library is the librarian. Librarians, by profession, are extremely knowledgeable and very helpful. Therefore, utilize their expertise throughout the literature search process.

SUMMARY

Stating a research problem is the first step in any research study. The research problem is often written as a question, but it can also be written in the form of one or more statements. In formulating a research problem the concepts must be clear, they must be such that they can be represented by evidence gained through direct observations or other more indirect methods, and it must be feasible to carry out such operations.

The process of defining a research problem can be thought of as an inverted triangle in which the scope of the study becomes increasingly narrow.

An important step that permeates the entire research process and is essential to the development of researchable problems is a review of the literature. A review of the literature serves the functions of (1) discovering findings from previous research on the general problem, (2) finding relevant theories that apply to the investigation being undertaken, and (3) informing the investigator of various methodologies and research procedures to study the problem.

The literature review begins in the library that includes numerous resources to assist the researcher. These include the card catalog, abstracts and indexes, journals, government documents, dissertations, theses, statistical data, and other reference materials.

CASE STUDY

Problem Definition, Use of Literature,
Independent and Dependent Variables,
Hypotheses, and Operational Definitions

Rosenblatt, A., & Kirk, S. A. (1981, spring). Cumulative effect of research courses on knowledge and attitudes of social work students. *Journal of Education for Social Work, 17*(2), 26-34.

In this research study the authors collected questionnaire data from undergraduate, masters, and doctoral students in fifteen social work programs across the country. The purpose of the study was to assess the cumulative effect of taking research courses on knowledge (how much did students understand about basic research methods?) and attitudes (did students think that research was important, useful, and valid?).

In order to define their research questions, and to ensure that their work would add to the existing knowledge base, the authors searched the literature on the research knowledge and attitudes of social work students. Although they found little theory to guide them, there were some interesting findings in the literature.

It seemed that not very much was known about the effectiveness of social work research courses in educating students about research methods. However, results of the five or six studies that had been done, indicated that masters' students did not learn much research, despite the requirement that they take at least one research course. Almost no study had been made of bachelors and doctoral students. Although these two groups have been small in the past, today they make up a large segment of social work education, so it was important to include them in a study on the effect of research courses.

The researchers defined two independent variables: level of education (which took on the values of bachelors, masters, and doctoral), and the number of research courses taken. The researchers were wise to measure the independent variable in these two different ways. Since social work programs vary in the number of required research courses, simply measuring the level of the student (bachelors, masters, or doctorate) may not be an accurate indicator of just how much research has been taught to them. The purpose of the study then, was to examine the effect of the level of education and the number of courses on the dependent variables.

The researchers chose to define four dependent variables. They were (1) level of knowledge of research methods, (2) belief that research is important, (3) belief that research is useful, and (4) conviction that existing research is valid.

The hypothesis of this study was that among social work students, as the level of education and number of research courses increase, knowledge of, and favorable attitudes toward, research will increase. In effect this study tests eight hypotheses by pairing each of two independent variables with each of four dependent variables:

Independent Variables	Dependent Variables
—level of education	—knowledge of research
—number of research courses	—importance
	—usefulness
	—conviction of validity

The researchers provided careful and detailed operational definitions for each of the independent and dependent variables. In each case the variable was defined by some response or set of responses that students made on a sixteen-page questionnaire that was distributed to the fifteen schools of social work. The level of education and the number of research courses are operationalized according to students' responses to two questions soliciting this information.

The researchers developed a sixty-item true and false inventory to measure knowledge of research. They first collected a pool of 120 knowledge items from existing research inventories, from research exams, and from research instructors. They pretested these items on a group of students. Those items that were answered correctly by over 80% of students were dropped because these items did not do a good job of differentiating knowledgeable students from those who were not. The remaining items were submitted to four research instructors. Items that were not answered correctly by all the instructors were dropped. Some final editing produced the completed knowledge inventory of 60 items. In scoring the inventory the student received one point for each correct item. Each student then could receive a score from 0 to 60, with a higher score indicating greater research knowledge.

The three attitude dependent variables were also operationally defined as the sum of students' responses to a series of questions (when answers are summed or averaged across items, the series of questions is referred to as a scale). Each attitude variable was measured by using three to seven questionnaire items. Each item was a simple declarative sentence to which the student was asked to respond by indicating a number from 1 to 6, with 1 indicating "Strongly Agree" and 6, "Strongly Disagree." For example, a typical item among those used to measure belief regarding importance of research was: "Limited agency resources should not be spent to pay for evaluative research." One item to measure belief in the usefulness of research was: "Generally, a researcher's interests are not related to the practice needs of social work."

These operational definitions illustrate two important features: (1) A great deal of effort is often put into operationally defining research variables. The operational definitions must be detailed and specific so that they are valid and reliable, that is, so they measure what they purport to measure and that they do it consistently. (2) In much human service research we rely on subjects' self-report. The questionnaire is the most common type of self-report and our research variables are often operationally defined as responses to a particular questionnaire item or set of items.

By the way, you may be wondering what the researchers found in this study. Unlike earlier studies that showed social work education did not lead to greater research knowledge, this study showed significant changes as the result of social work education. As the level and amount of education increased, students' knowledge level and their belief in the importance and usefulness of research increased. However, bachelors, masters, and doctoral students did not differ in the extent to which they believed that currently available research was valid.

Chapter 4

SAMPLING

Suppose we have defined a problem to be researched. We have looked at the relevant literature to see what theory and what data are available to guide us. On the basis of this knowledge we have set out hypotheses to be tested, and have operationally defined the concepts and variables in our hypotheses to make this test possible. What next?

Before we can collect our data or observations we need to decide which individuals, families, groups, organizations, communities, or events we will study. In other words, what *sample* will we choose?

In a sense, each of us collects data all the time, data in the form of unsystematic observations about the world. For example, have you ever heard any of the following statements?

- Most people on welfare are lazy.
- Social workers are "do-gooders."
- Old people are rigid.
- Adolescents today have no respect for authority.

These statements are conclusions based on a sort of sampling. We observe welfare recipients or social workers or others, and based on our observations we draw conclusions about these groups. These "common sense" conclusions are often inaccurate because our samples are too limited or too biased. For instance, our "sample" of welfare recipients may be limited to several recipients who engaged in fraud and were written up in the local newspapers. Newspapers are not systematic or inclusive about which welfare recipients they write stories about. In fact, the sample they present to the public is likely to be limited to those recipients who have done something wrong.

Viewed in this way it is easy to understand why samples of behavior based on personal experience are not very good for understanding what groups are really like. The purpose of scientific sampling is to generate samples that *do* give us an accurate understanding of what groups and individuals are like.

SOME TERMS

Definition: A *population* is the collection of all individuals, families, groups, organizations, communities, events, and so on that we are interested in finding out about.

In order to define a population we specify a set of variables or characteristics. For example, I might be interested in studying persons 65 years of age or older. My population would then be all individuals in the United States (or other specified area) who are 65 or older. Or, my population might be defined as all females 65 or older currently living in a nursing home facility. Or, it might be all mthers with children under the age of 5 who work at least ten hours per week outside the home.

Definition: Each member (person, family, organization, event, and so on) of a population is called an *element* of that population. When data are presented based on a measurement of each population element (say, individual test scores for students in a school population), the element is also referred to as a *unit of analysis.*

Populations tend to be very large. For this reason researchers rarely study every element in the population. Rather, they select a portion of that population for study.

Definition: A *sample* is a portion of a population selected for study.

Sometimes populations are defined in very concrete terms, as in the example of all persons 65 and over in the United States. At times, however, researchers are not as clear as they should be about the specific characteristics that define the population. In a study that uses college students to evaluate the effectiveness of an Assertion Training program, what is the population? Is it all students at the researcher's university? All students at the researcher's university who volunteer for a training program? Or is it all college-aged men and women? Most likely, the researcher would like to be able to say that his or her program was effective for all young adults, so that the last definition of the population would be the most appropriate.

It is important to state the specific variables or characteristics that define our population. Even though constraints of time and money prevent us from actually compiling a list of all elements of the population, if we have clearly defined our population, we should be able to describe how this could be done if we had the resources.

Why use samples? In most cases our interest goes beyond the limited number of elements we are studying. We are really interested in making statements about characteristics of the population, or statements about how variables are related in the population. We say that we seek to "generalize our (sample) findings to the population." Is Assertion Training effective with young adults? What impact does availability of in-home care have on older persons in this country? Are men really more sexist than women? What characteristics do the most effective school teachers have?

If we could measure every element in the population we would surely have answers to our research questions. But populations are very large. For practical reasons it is usually impossible to study every element in the population. It would be too costly and many individuals, groups, and so on, would not be available for our interview, questionnaire, or observation.

The researcher resolves this problem by studying a sample and generalizing his or her findings from the sample to the population. This is the most efficient way to do research, since we have methods that allow us to estimate characteristics of populations by measuring only a small sample of population elements. Of course, we have to assume that the sample is representative of the population. Otherwise, what we find in the sample may not be true for the population. Later in this chapter we will discuss different methods for ensuring that our samples are representative of the populations to which we seek to generalize.

There are of course times when we want to sample every element of some population. This will be the case if the population is small enough so that every element can be measured without much additional cost. It will also be the case in situations where we are not interested in generalizing to some larger group. For example, the director of your agency may ask you to study staff morale within your agency. If the purpose of the research is to learn only about the situation in your particular agency (perhaps so that recommendations to improve morale could be drafted), then the collection of all staff members in your agency *is* the population. In this case the sample and the population are the same.

RANDOMNESS AND REPRESENTATIVENESS

Randomness and representativeness are two characteristics of samples and sampling plans.

> Definition: *Random sampling* is a procedure for drawing a sample from a population so that every element in the population has an equal chance of being selected for the sample.

In most situations random sampling is the best way to select a sample. By introducing randomness into the selection of elements for the sample, we minimize our biases and other systematic factors that may make the sample different from the population from which it was drawn. For example, if the authors wanted to study public attitudes toward funding of social welfare programs they might be tempted to interview those people who were most convenient—students, friends, relatives—rather than to interview individuals randomly selected from the population. But this sample is almost certainly biased. The authors' acquaintances are likely to be more educated and more "liberal" on social issues than the population at large. Results based on this sample would be inaccurate for the population.

There is another reason for using random sampling. After data collection, we apply statistical tests to infer the characteristics of populations based on characteristics of the sample. (For example, if the mean income of sample respondents was $12,000, we can infer what the mean income of all persons in the population is likely to be.) In order to use such statistical tests we must assume that the sample was randomly selected from the population.

> Definition: A *representative sample* is one that is very similar to the population from which it is drawn, on those variables relevant to the study.

Variables relevant to the study include the dependent variable or variables (for instance, assertiveness), as well as all variables that might be related to the dependent variable (such as age, sex, and race). So, in a survey of social science majors, if the population of all currently enrolled social science majors is 55% female, 82% white, and has an average age of 25 years, then a representative sample of social science majors should have approximately the same distribution of these variables.

Are random samples representative of the populations from which they are drawn? It turns out that random sampling is only one way of constructing representative samples, and it does not always produce truly representative samples.

However, random samples *tend* to be representative. This is due to a natural process called the "principle of randomization," which can be understood intuitively. Since, in random sampling, every element of the population has an equal chance of being selected, elements with certain characteristics—male or female, high or low income, and so on—will, if selected, probably be counterbalanced in the long run by selection of other elements with the "opposite" quantity or quality of the characteristic. Characteristics that are most typical of the population are those that occur most frequently, and they are therefore most likely to be selected for the sample. (For example, if I have twice as many women as men students in my class, and if I randomly select a sample or subgroup of students from this class, this sample is also likely to have about a two to one female to male ratio.)

Although random samples tend to be representative, and although random sampling is usually the best way to get a representative sample, there is no guarantee that random sampling will produce a representative sample. In the female-dominated classroom for instance, if my sample is small, say just a few students, the chances that the sample will mirror the 2:1 sex ratio of the class (population) are much smaller than if my sample were large. Large random samples are more likely to be representative than are small samples. Large samples allow the principle of randomization to work. In small samples, a few individuals with nonrepresentative characteristics can make the sample less representative.

(You can verify this principle by repeatedly flipping a coin and noting the proportion of heads and tails. If you flip the coin just four or five times, the proportion of heads may be quite far from .50. If you flip the coin 25 or 100 times, the proportion of heads is much more likely to be close to the true proportion of .50.)

RANDOM SAMPLING
VERSUS RANDOM ASSIGNMENT

In situations where we are studying multiple subjects we typically use the process of randomization at two different points in the research. It is important to distinguish between these two independent steps.

The first step is to select randomly those individuals or elements from the population that will be included in the study, that is, to select the sample. The next step is to assign those individuals or elements randomly to different conditions. Some subjects may be assigned, for instance, to receive a treatment, while the remaining subjects might be placed in a control group. In most situations it is desirable to use the process of randomization for both sample selection and assignment to comparison conditions. It is not always possible to do this. Still, there are many situations where you will be able to select a sample randomly and randomly assign individuals to different conditions. Let's see how this is done.

Imagine that you did so well in your research course that the Friendly Family Service Society of North America has decided to hire you as Chief Evaluator. Your job is to determine if family therapy is effective. You decide that you want to answer this question by dividing a number of client families into two groups of equal size: families in one group will receive the Friendly Family Therapy program (treatment group); families in the other group will meet regularly with a therapist, but the therapist will not provide any specific therapy interventions (control group). Then at the end of the ten-week Family Therapy program you will evaluate all the families to see how well they are functioning.

You ask directors of all member agencies to submit to you a list of all families currently on the waiting list for Family Therapy. When you assemble all the names you find that you have a computer printout with 5,000 names. Since you have only enough resources to study 40 families, you decide on 40 as your sample size. Half of these families will receive Friendly Family Therapy and half will not. (Because you are an ethical human service worker, you make sure that at the end of the evaluation all families who did not receive therapy will be offered the service.) In other words, your task is to draw a random sample of 40 families from a population of 5,000 families, and then to randomly assign the 40 families in equal numbers to two comparison groups.

Where do you begin? Start by numbering the families on your

printout from 0001 to 5000. In order to choose 40 randomly selected families you will have to refer to a random numbers table. We have reproduced a portion of such a table below. You should begin at a randomly selected point in the table and read off four digits at a time, vertically or horizontally. (You can find a randomly selected point in the table by closing your eyes and stabbing the page with your pencil. Do be careful to keep your hand out of the way.)

.	.	.	.	.
.	.	.	.	.
.	.	.	.	.
.	.	.	.	.
..41995	88931	73631	69361	05375....
..10798	86211	36584	67466	69373....
.	.	.	.	.
.	.	.	.	.
.	.	.	.	.
.	.	.	.	.

In this example we read off four digits at a time horizontally. Note that the grouping of numbers in the table is arbitrary and is done only to make the table easier to read. Each group of four digits represents a family to be selected for our sample. Skipping numbers that are larger than 5000 we determine that:

Family 4199 is Subject 1
Family 5889 is skipped
Family 3173 is Subject 2
Family 6316 is skipped
Family 9361 is skipped
Family 0537 is Subject 3, . . . and so on

Stop when you have selected 40 subjects. You now have a random sample of 40 families drawn from a population of 5,000 families. The next step is to assign families randomly, 20 each, to the Therapy and Control conditions. We could use the four-digit Family numbers again, but to make things easier we renumber the families from 01 to 40. Again we enter the Random Numbers Table at another randomly selected point, and this time we read off pairs of digits:

.
.
.

| ..... 34803 | 92479 | 33399 | 71160 | 64777 | 83378 | ..... |
| ..... 68553 | 28639 | 96455 | 34174 | 11130 | 91994 | ..... |

.
.
.

Using the same procedure as last time we select Families 34, 39, 24, 33, and so on until we have selected 20 of our 40 families. Then we randomly decide if these 20 families will be the Therapy or the Control condition. We can do this by flipping a coin. Or, if we want to be more sophisticated, we can specify that this group will be the Treatment group if the first number randomly selected from the table is odd, or the Control group, if it is even. The remaining 20 families are assigned to the other condition. (If we have more than two groups we could number them 1, 2, 3, and so on, and then assign them to the conditions in the order in which these numbers appear in the Random Numbers Table, skipping out of range numbers.)

In our discussion of the principle of randomization we said that random samples tend to be representative of the populations from which they are drawn. The principle of randomization results in a related phenomenon: If sample elements are randomly assigned to groups, the groups will tend to be equivalent. This means that comparison groups formed by random assignment should be very similar to each other on variables such as sex, race, age, and so on.

Just as random sampling does not guarantee a representative sample, random assignment to groups does not *guarantee* equivalent groups. The larger the groups, the more likely they will be similar. The same principle is at work. If the groups are small, a few atypical elements may make a group different from the others. But with large groups, any atypical element assigned to one group is likely to be counterbalanced in the other groups, and population characteristics are more likely to be reflected equally in each of the comparison groups. When we study group research designs in the next chapter, we will see that the equivalence of comparison groups is important in many studies.

TYPES OF SAMPLES

Researchers try to select samples that are representative of the populations from which they are drawn so that they can make statements about those populations, based on their study of the samples. In most situations it would be ideal to draw random samples of sufficient size from our populations because these samples are most likely to be representative. However, human service researchers are usually limited by real world constraints such as little money, inaccessible or unwilling subjects, and lack of information about populations. In the face of these constraints, a number of sampling procedures have been developed. We will review the most common ones.

There are two types of samples.

Definition: *Nonprobability samples* are those that do not use random sampling. *Probability samples* are those that use random sampling in at least one stage of the sampling process.

NONPROBABILITY SAMPLING

Accidental sampling is the weakest form of sampling. In this procedure subjects are recruited as they become available or because they happen to be convenient for the researcher. Such samples are often limited to personal contacts of the researchers, or to people who happen to be available at meetings or in organizations, or in a particular place and time. A favorite type of sample used by college professors is the professor's own class: It's handy and the professor has a captive sample, so to speak.

This is a weak form of sampling because it does nothing to control bias. For example, suppose we wanted to study the attitudes of students at the University of Hard Knocks toward a recent proposal to use mandatory student fees to build a campus swimming pool. We decide to distribute a brief questionnaire to students by setting up a booth in the student union and asking passersby to complete and return it to us.

This is an accidental sample because it includes only those students who happen to walk by our booth *and* are willing to fill out our questionnaire. The sample is likely to be biased on certain variables that are related to attitudes toward the swimming pool proposition. It is probably biased against working students and those who live off campus, since these students are less likely to be in the union. They are also less likely to want to pay for a pool. The sample is probably biased against disabled students for the same reasons. It is also limited to those students with the strongest opinions on the subject, since they are most likely to have the motivation to complete and return the questionnaire. The problem in using this sample is that it is not a good base from which to make generalizations about the attitudes of all students at the University.

Quota sampling attempts to avoid at least some of the biases of accidental sampling. In this procedure the researcher has some knowledge about characteristics of the population likely to affect the dependent variables—characteristics such as age, race, and sex. This knowledge is then used to establish quotas for the numbers of persons with the relevant characteristics that must be included in the sample. So, for example, if we wanted to construct a quota sample of human service students, we begin by looking at national statistics on the characteristics of human service students. If our national data tell us that human service students are 65% female, 84% white, and that 58% are 25 years of age and under, we select students for our sample so that it will have the same proportions of students with these characteristics. Specifically, our data collectors will be instructed to recruit a certain number of white females under 25, a certain number of black females under 25, and so on.

It is not always necessary to select individuals in numbers proportional to their presence in the population. For example, we may know that there are two females for each male in the population, but we do not have a sufficient number of females available to us to include twice as many females as males in our sample. The sex ratio in our sample may be 1:1. In that case we can simply weight the females' responses by two so that the final result will reflect the correct (population) proportions. The only requirement is that we sample enough of each kind of student so that some confidence can be placed in the results.

Most commonly there are few restrictions on the particular persons that can be chosen for the sample as long as they fulfill the needed quota. Some public opinion polls use this procedure, setting quotas for the variables most likely to be related to opinions on public issues—sex, race, income level, and geographical location.

It is possible of course to set certain restrictions on interviewers or other data collectors so that the most obvious biases are avoided. So, if you are surveying low-income families, you can require your interviewers to use in-person interviews so that those without a phone are not excluded, to interview a certain number of families who live on upper floors (to counteract interviewers' aversion to climbing stairs), and so on. Other than that, in quota sampling, interviewers are free to choose whomever they wish for the sample, provided that they fulfill the specified quota.

Still, quota sampling represents only a marginal improvement over accidental sampling. In fact, within each class set up by the quota (e.g., black females under 25 years of age) we are actually taking an accidental sample. Quota sampling is an improvement over accidental sampling in that its use of quotas "forces" the sample to be representative of the population, at least on a few of the most obvious variables. The limitation of the quota sample is that it is not truly representative. There are a multitude of other variables that may be related to what you are studying, and that may or may not be reflected accurately in the sample. These variables are usually not known.

The *purposive sample* is another type of sample that does not use randomization in its selection of elements. It is similar to the quota sample, but it does not use specific predetermined quotas. In this method subjects are hand picked by the researchers in order to serve the purpose of the particular study. For example, suppose I designed a curriculum for a program to train child welfare workers how to detect and treat child abuse. In order to judge the quality and appropriateness of the curriculum I want to submit it to a number of child abuse experts and ask them to complete a questionnaire on their opinions of the curriculum. This is a situation in which I may want to hand pick the members of my sample. I will use my judgment and knowledge of the field to identify persons whom I feel to be leaders and experts in this area.

Purposive samples have also been used to predict the outcome of elections. In this situation the researcher hand picks a few key election districts and samples voters in those districts on their anticipated voting pattern. This is sometimes a good method for predicting an election, particularly if the researcher can identify election districts that have consistently mirrored the results for the entire area or state.

From a research point of view nonprobability samples are less desirable than probability samples. Because they do not use randomization in their selection of elements they are often seriously biased, many times in ways that make their findings suspect or invalid. Certainly, wherever possible the probability samples that are described below should be preferred. There are, however, reasons for using non-probability samples in some situations.

There may simply be no other way to study the phenomenon at hand. For example, a group of researchers studied the norms and behaviors of an urban youth gang. Since these gang members were extremely wary of outsiders, the researchers chose to study only the gangs with which they were involved. In fact, they spent many months interacting with, and getting the trust of, gang members before they collected any data. Since these were the only gang members available to them it was simply a question of studying this accidental sample or not studying gangs at all. The anthropologist is often in a similar situation. In studying a dying culture, for instance, the researcher will have to rely on available respondents.

Another situation in which a nonprobability sample is appropriate is when the researcher's purpose is not to generalize to a population. That is, the researcher has some purpose other than making accurate statements about the distribution of certain variables in a population. In our discussion of purposive sampling we gave one such example, in which the researcher hand selected a sample of child abuse experts to judge a training curriculum. Here the purpose was to judge the quality of the curriculum, rather than to generalize to a population.

The senior author studied older gay men to determine if they fit the stereotypes that are associated with this group: that they are lonely, isolated, and poorly adjusted (Berger, 1984). Almost all research on homosexuality must rely on nonprobability samples because it is difficult to define, locate, and recruit this population for study. Suppe (1982) defended this use of a nonprobability sample on the following grounds. To the extent that the purpose of the study was to refute commonly held stereotypes about older gay men (rather than to describe the characteristics of this population as a whole), the use of a nonprobability sample is appropriate, as long as it is sufficiently large and includes a sufficient diversity of respondents.

Although researchers would often prefer to use probability samples, much human service research has used nonprobability samples. This research has often added important new knowledge to the literature.

PROBABILITY SAMPLING

The most basic type of sampling is *simple random sampling*. In many cases it is the most desirable, if not the most feasible, form of sampling,

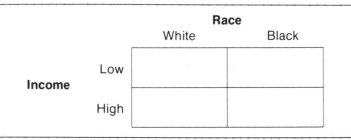

Figure 4.1 Illustration of a Stratified Sample Using the Variables of Race and Income to Define Strata

and it is used as a component of other probability sampling procedures.

In a simple random sample every element of the population has an equal chance of being selected into the sample. The list of forty families from the Friendly Family Service Agency that we generated earlier is a simple random sample.

Although simple random sampling produces unbiased samples—that is, the samples are likely to be representative of the population—it is not always the most efficient method for our research purpose.

In a *stratified sample* (also called a stratified random sample) the population is divided into subgroups or strata by population character-istics such as race, income, and sex. A simple random sample is then drawn for each subgroup or stratum. For example, if researchers wanted to stratify their population on the basis of race and income, they would set up the table of cells illustrated in Figure 4.1. They would then draw a simple random sample within each of the cells, that is, from low-income whites, then from low-income blacks, and so on.

When is a stratified sample preferable to a simple random sample? In general, stratified sampling will be more efficient than simple random sampling when stratifying the sample results in homogeneous subgroups. Homogeneous subgroups occur when, on the dependent variables, there are fewer differences within groups (say, low-income blacks) than between groups. In other words, in a stratified sample, the differences between subgroups should be large in comparison to differences within subgroups.

Once we have defined our strata there are two ways in which we can sample. In *proportional stratified sampling* the number of elements sampled in each subgroup is proportional to its representation in the population. So, for example, if low-income blacks make up 8% of the population, then 8% of the elements in the total sample will be low-income blacks. (It is of course also possible to select different numbers within subgroups and to weight the scores in the subgroups so that they reflect the relative sizes of subgroups in the population. As in quota sampling, this may be necessary if the researcher cannot get a sufficient number of subjects for each of the subgroups so that they reflect the population proportions.)

In *nonproportional stratified sampling* an equal number of elements is selected for each subgroup, or elements are selected in numbers that do not reflect their proportions in the population.

Proportional stratified sampling is used when the researcher wants to generalize his or her findings to the population as a whole. In this case the goal is to produce a sample that is as representative of the population as possible. To the extent that we have included important subgroups in the same proportions as in the populations, we have guaranteed that our sample is similar to the population, at least on the stratified variables.

There are, however, times when the researcher will want to use nonproportional sampling. One such situation is when the researcher's purpose is not to generalize to the population as a whole, but rather to make comparisons among subgroups. For example, if the researcher is interested in comparing the job opportunities of blacks and whites it makes sense to include an equal number of blacks and whites in the sample, even though they are not equal in number in the population.

Another situation calling for the use of nonproportional sampling is when the researcher wants to ensure that representatives of an important but very small subgroup within a population are included in the sample. For instance, a simple random sample of refugee families may fail to include Kampuchean refugees. If the researcher wants to ensure that this group will be studied, the researcher can do so by including them in numbers greater than their proportional representation in the population.

Finally, nonproportional stratified sampling is also appropriate when the researcher is interested in subdividing cases within strata for further analysis. In Figure 4.1, for example, the researcher may want to do additional analyses to study the differences within the subgroup of low-income blacks: What are the differences, say, between urban and rural low-income blacks? Or between low-income blacks who live alone versus those who are heads of household? In this case it would be best to have equal subsamples of sufficient size for each of the strata.

One limitation in the use of stratified samples should be noted. As we increase the number of variables on which we stratify, we increase the number of cells in our sampling design, requiring larger samples in order to fill up the cells. This is particularly important when we want to compare different subgroups or cells, because cells with very few elements will generally not give good estimates.

As we add variables on which to stratify, the number of cells increases dramatically. In Figure 4.1, for example, if we were to add just one additional stratifying variable with just two values, say, sex of respondent, the number of cells would double. So it is a good idea to remember that we should stratify only on those variables that will result in homogeneous groups. If there is no reason to believe that stratifying will lead to more homogeneous groups, then it is more efficient to use a simple random sample.

Simple random sampling and stratified sampling are usually the best ways to ensure representative samples. But, alas, they are not always possible. They were designed to meet the needs of statisticians rather than researchers, who must deal with real world limitations. For instance, we may not be able to draw a simple random sample because we are unable to generate a list of all the elements in the population. If we were studying elementary school children in North America, for instance, how would we get a list of all school children so that we could draw our random sample from it? We certainly don't have the resources to contact every school district in our population, even assuming they would all cooperate. And even if we did obtain a fairly complete list, it is unlikely we would have the resources to send our interviewers to schools scattered all over the country. That wouldn't be efficient, since there might be only one or two respondents in any particular school.

These are some reasons why alternatives to simple random sampling have been developed. The most common alternative, and one used frequently for large-scale surveys, is *cluster sampling*. In this method the population is divided into clusters or units, and then into successively smaller subunits. At each level the units and subunits are randomly selected. Clusters are usually defined as geographical or organizational units. For example, in a study of high school students' attitudes toward birth control, I may use cluster sampling in order to obtain results that I can say are indicative for students in my state. I randomly select a number of state regions, then within each selected region I randomly select a number of counties, within each county I randomly select a number of school districts, and so on. The last cluster level may be the individual classroom.

Within each unit I may take a simple random sample of subunits, or if the number of elements in a subunit is small, I may include all the elements in my sample. In the birth control study, for example, if there are only one to five high schools in a school district, I may sample all the high schools for each selected school district. Within the classroom I may ask all or some students to complete a questionnaire.

Although a simple random sample or a stratified sample may yield more precise results, its use must be weighed against its cost. In the birth control study, for example, it would be very expensive to compile a list of all students in the population, and to contact the many widely scattered schools that would be reflected in a random selection of students. And once we got access to the classroom, our simple random sample would require that we sample only one or a few students, while we could have easily included the entire class without much additional effort. In fact, administering questionnaires to a few selected students may very well be more disruptive than administering them to the entire class.

Cluster sampling avoids these problems. It limits the number of schools we would have to approach and it allows us to collect data from all the students who may be conveniently available. The resources we save can then be applied to collecting a larger sample, making cluster sampling a practical alternative to simple random sampling.

A final form of probability sampling is *systematic sampling*. In this procedure the first sample element is randomly chosen from the numbers 1 through K, and subsequent elements are chosen at every Kth interval. For example, a systematic sample of homes may be selected from a suburban neighborhood. If there are ten houses on each block, I set K = 10 and I use a Random Numbers Table to choose a number between 01 and 10 (by picking the first two digits between 01 and 10 after my pencil lands on a randomly selected point on the page). If K = 6, I include the sixth home on each block within my sample, that is, I interview the families in homes 6, 16, 26, 36, and so on, until I reach the desired sample size.

In systematic sampling it is critical that the first element between 1 and K be chosen randomly. If it is not, then most of the elements in the population have no chance at all for selection into the sample, and the sample cannot be assumed to even approximate a simple random sample.

Systematic samples are used primarily for convenience and simplicity. For instance, the senior author once participated in telephone survey of community attitudes toward the local United Way. A phone survey, of course, excludes many low-income people who do not have phones, but within that constraint we did have a list of population elements: the telephone directory. It would have been possible, but impractical, to take a simple random sample from the phone book. It would have required numbering tens of thousands of names, and the process of picking out corresponding numbers from a Random Numbers Table would have been tedious.

We chose a simple alternative. Based on the number of telephone listings and the number of respondents we wanted to include, we determined our K. We then randomly selected a number between 1 and K. In this way we determined that every sixteenth name in every third column of listings should be included in our sample. By using a specially marked card it was possible to select the appropriate name on each page quickly. Each of these listings was called and the first adult to answer was asked to participate in our brief telephone interview.

There is a very serious limitation to systematic sampling. If there is any systematic or cyclical bias in the population, a systematic sample may also be seriously biased. In the telephone survey it didn't seem likely that there were characteristics common to persons whose names were listed in the sixteenth position in every third column, or that these persons differed consistently from the other listings.

But consider the survey of suburban homes. Our sample of every sixth home on each block is seriously biased. This sample excludes homes on corner lots. Although you might not think that this factor is related to what you are studying, consider again. Research studies have shown that families who live in corner homes are different from their neighbors: These homes are more expensive and their occupants are likely to have higher incomes and more conservative political beliefs. It is easy to imagine a number of phenomena that would be affected by this sample bias: attitudes toward social welfare programs, voting preference, and so on.

It is always possible that a systematic sample may be biased because of this kind of systematic or cyclical characteristic in the population. Since systematic samples are always constructed from lists of elements, whenever a systematic sample is possible, it should also be possible to draw a simple random sample or stratified sample. Unless the additional work is prohibitive, you should use the latter types of samples.

SUMMARY

In observing the world around us we all use a sort of commonsense sampling. But because this sampling is unsystematic it often results in wrong conclusions. The scientific method relies on the careful selection of elements of populations into samples, so that these samples can be used as the basis for generalizations about the populations from which they were drawn. The most basic form of sampling is simple random sampling, in which each element of the population has an equal chance of being selected for the sample. A sample selected in this way will tend to be representative of the population. In addition to the selection of a random sample from a population, many studies also use random assignment to comparison groups. All sampling plans can be divided into nonprobability samples (which do not use random sampling) and probability samples (which use random sampling in at least one step of the sampling plan).

CASE STUDY

Sampling

Deimling, G. T., & Bass, D. M. (1986). Symptoms of mental impairment among elderly adults and their effects on family caregivers. *Journal of Gerontology, 41*(6), 778-784.

It has been known for some time that family members who provide significant amounts of care to an impaired elderly person often feel burdened and experience stress. This study was designed to examine the causes of stress on caregivers of impaired elderly persons. Specifically, the study analyzed the effects of the elderly's level of social functioning, disruptive behaviors, and cognitive incapacity (e.g., memory loss, forgetfulness, confusion) on the amount of stress experienced by the caregiver.

The data used in this research came from a study of families who provided care to impaired elderly persons residing in their own homes in the Cleveland area. From over 2,000 referrals, 614 families were chosen using a stratified random sampling procedure. The sample was stratified into three subgroups: geographic area of residence, racial characteristics, and generational configuration (number of generations living in the household).

The subgroup of geographic area of residence included 40% urban, 40% suburban, and 20% rural; the racial characteristics included 25% black and 75% white; and the generational configuration included 50% one-generation, 30% two-generation, and 20% three-generation households.

Although the researchers did not state in detail how the original sample was drawn, they probably followed a procedure that resembled the following. Based on theory and previous research, the researchers expected that variations in caregiving occurred because of the geographic location (urban, suburban, or rural), race (white or black), and generational configuration of the family (one-, two-, or three-generational households). Therefore, because these variables were related to caregiver stress, they wanted to assure that these subgroups would be adequately represented in the sample. In addition, the researchers' ability to generalize their findings based on a sample of the population would be enhanced if the sample resembled the population on the stratified variables: geographic location, race, and generational configuration.

How did the researchers determine the proper proportions for each subgroup? The ideal way would have been to make the size of the sample subgroups proportional to the actual characteristics of caregivers in the Cleveland area population. (That is, if 40% of caregivers in the Cleveland area lived in suburban areas, then the sample would have been chosen so that 40% of caregivers in the sample lived in suburban areas.)

However, it is unlikely that the researchers had this information about the Cleveland area population. They did, however, have this information on the 2,000 plus families on their referral list. Therefore, they had to first take the 2,000 plus families and identify each according to its geographic area of residence, race, and generational configuration. They then randomly selected a sample of families so that the proportions of the sample within each stratum (urban, rural, suburban, white, black, one-, two-, and three-generational families) were similar to the proportions in the 2,000 plus families from which the sample was drawn. In this way, the researchers guaranteed that their sample of 614 families was similar to the referral list of 2,000 plus families on the stratified variables.

What did the researchers find? In the sample of 614 families, elderly care recipients averaged 78.2 years of age. Two-thirds were female. They had been receiving care from their spouse or children for an average of six years.

This research also contributed to our understanding of the causes of stress for caregivers of the impaired elderly. It is often assumed that cognitive incapacity (forgetfulness and confusion) is the cause of stress on caregivers. This study found that other factors—disruptive behavior and social functioning (the older person's level of cooperation, withdrawal, and isolation)—were more important sources of stress for caregivers.

Chapter 5

GROUP RESEARCH DESIGNS

Suppose we have selected our sample: the individuals, groups, or other elements that we wish to study. A plan is then needed to tell us how to carry out our study.

We need to know if the elements in our sample will be divided into groups, and, if so, how that will be done. If the study is experimental we need to know which group or groups will be exposed to our independent variable (say, a treatment program); if the study is nonexperimental we need to understand how the independent variable (say, race, sex, or occupation) affects the various groups in our study. We need to know who will be measured and at what times. We need to specify time order: When will measurement of individuals and exposure to the independent variable occur? And which, if any, events will occur simultaneously in the various groups?

Research designs are plans that provide answers to these questions.

NOTATION

Much of the material in this chapter is drawn from a little book published in 1963 by Donald T. Campbell and Julian C. Stanley: *Experimental and Quasi-Experimental Designs for Research.* This book, which has become a classic, is a basic reference resource for understanding all aspects of group research design. Campbell and Stanley developed a shorthand notation to describe research designs.

85

Since it would be very cumbersome to give a verbal description every time we wanted to specify a research design, this shorthand will prove invaluable.

According to this notation, "X" represents the exposure of an individual or group to an independent variable. In an experimental study the "X" is an event that is administered by the researcher to the subjects, such as exposure to a treatment program. In a nonexperimental study the "X" represents some event or characteristic, whose effect on subjects is to be studied. For instance, in a study of differences between blue-collar and white-collar workers, the "X" represents the "exposure" of subjects to blue-collar or white-collar status. These could be symbolized as "X_{BC}" and "X_{WC}," respectively.

"O" represents the measurement or observation of an individual or group. It is an event such as administering a test or questionnaire, or conducting an interview. It is the means by which the dependent variable is measured: It is a measure of the effect of "X." For instance, if "X" is a job training program, then "O" might be a measure of how many days the trainee has been employed, as determined by his responses to a questionnaire.

When "Xs" and "Os" appear in the same row, this means that they are applied to the same set of persons. Each row of symbols, then, represents a separate group. Time order is indicated by the position of the symbols, from left to right. "Xs" and "Os" vertical to one another occur at the same time.

As we saw in Chapter 4, comparison groups can be formed by random assignment. This is equivalent to writing each person's name on a slip of paper and randomly drawing names out of a hat. If there are two groups the first half of all names will go into one group and the remaining names into the other. The way this is actually done was described in Chapter 4.

In many instances comparison groups are not formed by random assignment. In the study comparing blue-collar and white-collar workers the two "groups" of workers already existed in the real world. In practical terms this means that the researcher did not assign individuals to belong to one group or the other, but merely asked each respondent regarding his or her occupational status. This is a very common research design and is referred to as an *intact groups* or *already formed groups* design.

When groups are formed by random assignment we indicate this by placing the letter "R" in front of each group. When groups are not formed by random assignment (intact groups is one such situation) then no "Rs" are used, but a dashed line is drawn to separate the groups.

For example, suppose we want to evaluate the effects of a reading comprehension program on the reading scores of elementary school children. "X" represents exposure to the reading program. "O" represents the administration of a reading test. Our school principal has allowed us to work with two classrooms, so we decide to run the reading program in one classroom and to use the other classroom as a control group. Our design might look like this:

X	O		Miss Wigly's class
	O		Miss Pigly's class

In this design we run our reading program in Miss Wigly's class, and when the program is finished we administer a reading test to all the students in both classes.

An alternative is to use comparison groups formed by random assignment. This, of course, presents many practical difficulties because the students will have to be placed into newly formed groups, different from their classroom groups. We would need to assign each student a number and then use the random numbers table to assign half the students to one, and half to the other group. Each group, then, will have some students from each of the classrooms and the design will look like this:

R	X	O
R		O

In these examples, tests (Os) were given after exposure to X, in this case the reading program. Tests or measurements given after exposure to the independent variable are called *posttests*. Tests or measurements given before exposure to the independent variable are called *pretests*. In the following examples two groups experience simultaneous pretests and posttests:

R	O	X	O		O	X	O
R	O		O		O		O

Below we have used notation to describe three additional designs. See if you can give a verbal description of each of these designs, and then refer to the verbal descriptions we have given to see if you were correct.

(a) R	O	X	O		(b) O	X	O
R	O	X	O		-----------------------		
					O		O

(c) R	O	X	O
R	O		O

R	O	X	O
R	O		O

(a) In this design a group of elements is randomly assigned to two groups. Both are pretested simultaneously and then one group is exposed to an independent variable or treatment. Sometime after this exposure, both groups are posttested simultaneously.
(b) In this design we have two groups not formed by random assignment. (They might be two classrooms, for instance.) Both are pretested simultaneously and then one group is exposed to an independent variable or treatment. Sometime after this exposure, both groups are posttested simultaneously.
(c) In this design we have four groups of elements or individuals. One group of individuals is randomly divided into two groups. Another, separate group of individuals is also randomly divided into two groups. All four groups are pretested simultaneously. Then one of the two randomly formed groups within each of the two original groups is exposed to an independent variable or treatment. Sometime after this exposure all four groups are posttested simultaneously.

These descriptions illustrate the usefulness of design notation: Notation allows us to describe designs clearly and efficiently. They prove the maxim that "a picture is worth a thousand words."

WHY IS RESEARCH DESIGN IMPORTANT?

Before getting into the specifics of research design we would like to present two examples that illustrate how important it is to understand basic principles of good design. In both examples the researchers came up with wrong conclusions because they used inappropriate designs.

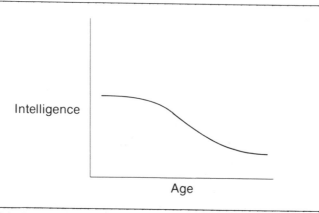

Figure 5.1   Graph Illustrating a Decline in Intelligence with Age

The first example comes from the research literature on aging. For many years gerontological researchers thought they had confirmed what many people believe: that intelligence declines with advanced age. They proposed the relationship between age and intelligence as seen in Figure 5.1.

This finding proved to be untrue. Later research indicated that there is little if any decline of verbal intelligence as people grow older (Edinberg, 1985, p. 16). (There is, however, a decline in psychomotor skills with increasing age.)

What happened? The original researchers had used an inappropriate design: a *cross-sectional design*. In this type of design the researchers measured the intelligence of different age cohorts (people of similar age) at the same point in time, for example, all 20-year-olds, all 30-year-olds, and so on:

X_{20} O

X_{30} O

X_{40} O

         . . . and so on

So each point on the graph in Figure 5.1 represents the average intelligence score of a *different* group of people.

The problem was this. The different age cohorts differed not only in age (the independent variable) but also in number of years of schooling. Older cohorts had fewer years of schooling than younger cohorts, because less education was available when these older folks were of school age. Persons with more years of schooling do better on all types of paper and pencil tests: They have more experience. In addition, for the younger cohorts the test-taking experience was more recent. Apparently, it was this difference in the amount of schooling and its effect on test taking (rather than the difference in age) that led to a difference in intelligence test scores.[1] (Later in this chapter we will refer to factors such as the differences in amount of education among groups as a bias due to selection.)

This was illustrated when researchers used a more appropriate research design: a *longitudinal design*. In this design the *same* group of individuals is followed over time and measured repeatedly to detect any changes in intelligence with age:

$$X \qquad O_{20} \qquad O_{30} \qquad O_{40} \qquad \dots \text{and so on}$$

It is easy to see why early researchers opted for the cross-sectional design. The longitudinal design requires much more effort because the researcher must keep track of individuals over a long period of time, and results are not available until after many years. However, the longitudinal design leads to a more accurate conclusion because differences among the "age groups" are due solely to age, and not to other factors such as differences in the amount of schooling. Therefore these other factors are not around to "contaminate" our results.

The second study to illustrate the importance of research design is hypothetical. In this example a family planning agency wishes to determine the most effective way to get couples to use birth control. A review of the literature and a look at programs used by other agencies suggest two strategies: television ads and a door-to-door educational campaign conducted by trained personnel. The literature suggests that personal contact, which is part of the door-to-door method, is the most powerful way to change public attitudes. However, the advantages of the door-to-door method must be weighed against its cost. It is a very expensive and time-consuming method. Television messages, while less powerful, reach a much larger audience. Given all these factors, the research question is "Which method will have the most impact on a community?"

The family planning researchers decide to test the two methods in two cities that they believe to be very similar. If this is true, then any differences in birth control practices or attitudes will be due to the different educational campaigns. For a period of six months, television ads are played on local stations in City A, while door-to-door visits are used in City B. The cities are in different parts of the country to ensure that couples in each city are exposed only to the campaign that is directed at that city. At the end of two years the birthrates are determined from records at the County Clerk's office in both cities. The design is as follows:

City A—TV Campaign	X_a	O_1
City B—Door-to-Door	X_b	O_2

Suppose that the researchers find that the birthrate is lower in City B at the conclusion of the study. Can they say with confidence that the door-to-door campaign was more effective in lowering the birthrate?

The answer is no. There are a number of weaknesses in the research design that make this conclusion suspect. Specifically, there are many factors *other than* the type of campaign (the independent variable) that could account for the lower birthrate in City B. Consider just a couple of examples.

We know that economic conditions are an important factor in couples' decisions to use birth control, but we don't know if economic conditions are similar in the two cities. What if a large factory closed in City B during the course of the study? The resulting unemployment and concern about economic conditions could be responsible for a lower birthrate in City B, even if there was no difference in the effectiveness of the two campaigns.

Here's another problem in interpreting the results. The researchers selected two cities that were similar. But it is never possible to select two areas that are exactly alike. Any differences in the type of people in the two towns could be responsible for the different birthrates, even if the two campaigns did not differ.

For instance, perhaps the lower birthrate in City B was due to the fact that residents of that city are older than those of City A and had a lower birthrate to begin with, or perhaps City B has more upwardly mobile families who want to limit family size. There are countless such variables that may have led to the difference in birthrates between the two cities.

Therefore, we cannot have much confidence that the difference was in fact due to the different campaigns.

This example illustrates the logic of research design. All research designs follow this logic, which can be described as follows: The goal of any research design is to show that the *experimental hypothesis* is correct. The experimental hypothesis is that "X" is responsible for the observed effect. In order to show that this is true, we have to rule out all *plausible alternative hypotheses*. These are a series of hypotheses that state that factors *other than* "X" are responsible for the observed effect.

In the family planning example, the experimental hypothesis is that the different educational campaigns are responsible for the different birthrates in the two cities. There are a series of plausible alternative hypotheses: that the closing of a factory in City B, that the older ages of City B residents, and so on . . . that these factors are responsible for the difference in birthrates between the cities.

The purpose of research design is to set up a situation so that we can rule out plausible alternative hypotheses. If we can rule out all hypotheses that are plausible alternatives to the experimental hypothesis, then the experimental hypothesis must be true. Another way to say this is that if we have comparison groups that are equal in every way, except for the independent variable, then any resulting differences between the groups must be due to the independent variable. (So, for example, if City A and City B were exactly equal on all factors other than the presence of two types of educational campaigns, then any subsequent differences that we find must be due to the difference in educational campaigns.)

To the extent that we have ruled out plausible alternative hypotheses we can say with confidence that we have shown that "X" was responsible for subsequent differences that we observe. When we have done this, we have established that our study has *internal validity*.

> Definition: *Internal validity* asks the question: Did the experimental treatment make a difference in this specific instance, with these subjects, in this setting, at this time?

When we conduct a research study we are teasing out the effect of an independent variable or variables on a dependent variable or variables. In other words, we are looking for an effect, such as the effect of an educational birth control campaign on subsequent birthrates. Our first order of business, of course, is to show that effect in the particular sample we are studying. In this case we want to show a difference in birthrates between City A and City B.

However, in most studies we would like to make statements about effects that apply beyond the particular sample we have studied. In the family planning study, for instance, we are almost certainly interested in finding the most effective educational medium so that it can be applied in other areas of the country, administered by different local groups, and using different personnel. We might also want our program to show an effect when its outcome is measured in different ways, say by measuring respondents' reported use of birth control, rather than the birthrate.

> Definition: *External validity* asks the questions: To what other groups of people, families, organizations, and the like can the observed effect be generalized? In what other settings and with what other treatment variables and outcome variables will this effect hold true?

The goal of every research design is to establish both internal and external validity. Internal validity is the first requirement of a research design because we must first establish that a particular effect occurs (such as the lowering of the birthrate due to an educational campaign). It is generally also desirable for our finding to have high external validity, that is, for our finding to be valid among other groups, in different settings, with other ways of implementing the treatment, and with other ways of measuring its effect.

Ideally, a good research design will be high in both internal and external validity. In this chapter we will evaluate a number of designs in terms of their internal and external validity. But first we must define a number of factors or threats to internal validity. Each of these factors represents a plausible alternative hypothesis, that is, a hypothesis that some factor other than "X" is responsible for an observed effect.

FACTORS OF INTERNAL VALIDITY

History refers to specific events, other than the experimental variable, that occur during the course of the study, and that may affect the outcome. In the family planning study, the closing of a factory in one of the cities was a factor of history. This event represents a plausible alternative hypothesis to the hypothesis that the difference in educational campaigns was responsible for the difference in birthrates between the cities. It is easy to understand that a factory closing will lead to economic problems that, in turn, might plausibly affect young families' desire to have children, and thus the birthrate.

We must always be attuned to events in the environment that may affect our studies, since the environment is constantly changing, and since research, especially human service research, is not conducted in a vacuum. Here is another example of a factor of history. Suppose we have developed a program of intensive services for the frail elderly with the goal of delaying or preventing placement in a nursing home. That is our "X." Our dependent variable is the length of time the individual continues to live at home.

Now suppose that during the course of the study the federal government implements Title XX, a law that provides money for services to keep people out of institutions for as long as possible. We cannot prevent our frail elderly clients from receiving other services, and to do so would be unethical. But this does present a problem for our research design. If our program "works," that is, if it is successful in keeping clients out of institutions, was it due to our program or to newly available Title XX services? Or was it due to the combination of the two? The implementation of Title XX, then, may be a plausible alternative hypotheses.

According to Campbell and Stanley (1963) *maturation* refers to "processes within the respondent operating as a function of the passage of time per se (not specific to the particular events), including growing older, growing hungrier, growing more tired and the like." For example, whenever we study the performance of young persons who are still growing and developing physically and mentally, we must take account of the fact that they are going to show performance changes (generally improvements) over time. This is due to maturation and would have occurred even without the experimental treatment.

For example, if I measure the reading achievement of a group of students in the fourth grade, and again when these students are in the sixth grade, there will probably be an increase in performance due solely to maturation. If we want to show that a reading improvement program increased achievement, we need to show an increase in scores above what would be expected from maturation alone.

Maturation also refers to decreases in ability over time. For example, suppose we used the following design to evaluate an activity program designed to increase the alertness and orientation of a group of frail elderly persons:

O_1 X O_2

At O_1 and O_2 we administer the Mental Status Quiz, a short questionnaire that measures orientation (it asks questions such as, "Can you name the two streets that form the nearest intersection?") (Goldfarb, 1962). We may find to our disappointment, that there is no change in mental status between O_1 and O_2. However, we need to take into account an important factor of maturation: The mental alertness of our subjects maybe declining over time. In the absence of our activity program there may have been a decrease in orientation at O_2. When we take maturation into account we may actually be able to say that our program was a success, despite a lack of change: The program was successful in preventing or slowing deterioration.

Another situation in which maturational effects are likely is when the experimental treatment or testing process is long enough for our subjects to tire. For example, if we test our subjects at the beginning and then again at the end of a long day of training, we have to consider that our subjects will probably be slowed down by fatigue.

Testing occurs whenever performance on a test is affected by having taken a previous test. The second test may or not be the same as the first test. It is very common, for example, for subjects to do better the second time they take a test that was the same or similar to an earlier test.

Think about the first time you took an academic aptitude test. It probably took some time to learn the ropes: to learn how to pace yourself, how to guess when you didn't know the answer, and how to fill in the bubbles on the computer answer sheet. Chances are that you will do better the second time around, simply because you are familiar with the process. You may also be more self-confident the second time around, and that will help your performance. Or, if you had a bad first experience you may actually be less confident the second time, and that will lower your performance. That too is an effect of testing.

In some situations there may be unintended changes over time in the way an effect is measured. This is a problem of *instrumentation*. A good analogy from the physical sciences is the change in calibration of a spring scale as it is used repeatedly. After weighing a number of heavy objects, the spring loosens enough to give inaccurate readings in subsequent weighings. That is why most spring scales have calibration adjustments, which allow the user to tighten the spring so that it is once again accurate. (Check your bathroom scale and you'll probably find one.)

Instrumentation problems in human service research are often more subtle and a bit harder to correct. An example of instrumentation comes from a study of the effectiveness of marital communication counseling in improving family interaction. Suppose that we measure our dependent variable, quality of communication, by placing each family in a room with a one-way mirror and asking them to hold a discussion in order to make a family decision, say, where to spend the next vacation. In an adjoining room behind the one-way mirror, we have placed an observer who has been trained to record one aspect of the quality of communication. Our observer records the frequency of positive statements ("I really like how you did that, sweetheart"), and negative statements ("That was dumb!").

When Mr. and Ms. Grumpy and their children Nasty and Hardly are given this assignment, they seem to take forever to come to a decision. Meanwhile, time is passing and, behind the mirror, our trusty observer is growing bored. Despite the observer's best intentions, he or she unwittingly changes the standard by which he or she judges whether a comment is positive. Perhaps the observer loosens up and judges a comment as positive, which he or she would previously have judged as neutral. This is an instrumentation problem. It is a problem because we would like to be certain that any changes in the quality of communication are due to our program, and not to an inconsistent (if well-meaning) observer. (The solution to this problem, by the way, is to have clear and specific operational definitions for the dependent variables, in this case, positive and negative communications, and to train our observers thoroughly.)

Statistical regression is a phenomenon that occurs with retesting of groups that have been selected because they have extreme scores. By extreme scores we mean scores that are either higher than average or lower than average. This is not an uncommon situation. For instance, in school settings we often select those children with the lowest performance scores to participate in remedial programs.

Regression refers to the fact that when such a group is retested, the average score at the second testing is likely to be closer to the mean score for the entire group. In other words, if we selected a group of low-scoring students and retested them, at the retest their average score would be somewhat higher than the average at the first testing. Two important things to keep in mind are that regression occurs only when groups are selected because they have extreme scores, and that regression is apparent for the group. It will not necessarily happen to an individual score.

An example of a situation in which regression is an important factor is the evaluation of the Head Start program. Head Start is a learning enrichment program for preschoolers. Head Start programs select children from families in areas where children have shown poor school performance in the past. In that sense, participants in Head Start are chosen precisely because they are from groups that tend to have low scores on tests of academic achievement. Consider the following design:

$$O_1 \quad X \quad O_2$$

"X" is participation in the Head Start program and O_1 and O_2 are pre- and posttests of academic performance. Because a regression effect is very likely in this situation, this is a poor design. If there is an increase in academic achievement at O_2 it may be due to regression, even if the Head Start program had no effect. It is also possible that regression and the program each contributed to a part of the increase at O_2, but there is no way in this design to separate the effect of these two factors.

Regression effects may also occur when subjects are retested on a test different from the original test. Campbell and Stanley (1963, p. 11) give the following example: "The principal who observes that his highest-IQ students tend to have less than the highest achievement-test scores (though quite high) and that his lowest-IQ students are usually not right at the bottom of the achievement-test heap (though quite low) would be guilty of the regression fallacy if he declared that his school is understimulating the brightest pupils and overworking the dullest." This hypothetical situation can be diagrammed as follows:

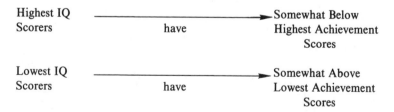

A statistical explanation for why regression occurs is beyond the scope of this text. But we can get an intuitive idea of what happens. Unlike the physical sciences, in human service research most of our measurements are imprecise. In other words, every measurement or observed score is composed of a theoretical "true" component and an "error" component, which is usually a relatively small positive or negative number. In other words, we assume that most of the time we are able to measure our concepts and variables accurately within a small margin of error—we may be a bit high or a bit low at each measurement. This can be expressed by the equation:

$$X_{observed} = X_{true} + X_{error}$$

When we choose only subjects with extreme scores, we are choosing those scores that are most likely to have large error components. When that extreme scorer was measured there happened to have been a large error component in the score. But since these errors are random, chances are that next time the score is measured its error component won't be as large. In other words, the retest score will be closer to the mean. When this happens to a set of retest scores, the average score will be closer to the mean.

Another factor of internal validity is *selection*. Selection problems occur when there are comparison groups and when the subjects in the groups differ on characteristics related to the dependent variable. When comparison groups are formed by random assignment of subjects to groups (as was illustrated in Chapter 4) then the groups will probably not differ on such characteristics. But when comparison groups are formed in any other way, such differences are common. It is often hard to know exactly how the groups differ and whether these differences might affect the outcome of the study.

For example, our family planning study above presented selection problems. Some selection factors (such as a higher proportion of older residents in City B) might certainly affect birthrates. Other ways in which the cities differed (say, differences in weather) may not. But it is always hard to tell. For instance, one of the authors' more impertinent students suggested that in cold weather people spend more time indoors and are thus more likely to engage in procreative activities. Thus a selection factor, which at first blush may not appear to be a plausible alternative hypothesis, may in fact be a plausible alternative to the experimental hypothesis (in this case that differences in birthrates between the two cities were due to the different educational campaigns).

Here is another common selection problem. Let's say that we believe that much of our current unemployment is due to the lack of skills of unemployed workers. We develop a six-week job training program and hypothesize that the program will result in higher employment levels for participants. These participants are recruited by placing a big sign in the Job Service office advertising our program. All workers who telephone us requesting the program are run through the one month of training. For our comparison group we randomly select an equal number of unemployed persons from the state's unemployment files. Our design looks like this:

X   O   Workers who request training

     O   Workers drawn from files

To measure the effect of our program we record the number of days of employment for workers in both groups for a period of six months after conclusion of the training. That is what the Os in our design represent. Suppose that at the end of the six-month follow-up we find that employment rates are higher for the trained group. Do we have cause for celebration? Did our training program work?

By now, you have probably learned to be more cautious. We cannot tell if our program was effective in increasing employment of trained workers. The problem is that a factor of selection may be responsible for the difference in employment rates, even if the program had no effect. Remember how we recruited workers for the training group? Workers in the training group were volunteers: Among all unemployed workers they were the only ones to take the initiative to respond to our ad. In this situation, and in many others, volunteers are very different from nonvolunteers. They are usually more motivated, better educated, and more skilled, and they are the most likely to succeed even if they receive no help. In our study we were comparing these sorts of people with others who did not volunteer. Therefore, the trained group may have been more successful because of their personal characteristics, even if the training program was completely useless.

Mortality is the final factor of internal validity that must concern us. Mortality results when we have comparison groups and when subjects drop out of these groups. Even if the groups were comparable before the dropout, once dropout occurs we can no longer be certain that the groups are comparable. If only a very few subjects drop out of the study relative to the size of the groups, this is probably not a serious problem. Some researchers have argued that if equal numbers of subjects drop out of comparison groups that mortality is not a problem, because equal dropout rates equalize the groups. This is not good thinking. For example, consider the following example.

Suppose that we again want to evaluate the effectiveness of job training on subsequent employment rates. But this time we select a number of unemployed workers and randomly assign equal numbers to two comparison groups. Given the random assignment we can feel comfortable in assuming that the groups are indeed comparable. (We'll assume that everyone we have selected agrees to participate.)

In the first group we run our standard one-month job training program. Now, it turns out that this is a very difficult program: it requires many hours of classroom contact, numerous take home assignments, and so on. We wonder whether we would not be just as successful if the program were less difficult. So we design an "easy" job training program, with fewer classroom hours, and more fun assignments. We run this program with our second group of unemployed workers:

$$R \quad X_{hard} \quad O$$
$$R \quad X_{easy} \quad O$$

Alas, this time we find that a sizable (but equal) number of workers have dropped out of both groups. Since the number of dropouts was equal can we still assume that our groups are comparable? If the remaining workers in the hard training group had higher employment rates, can we conclude that the hard program was more effective than the easy program?

Since equal numbers dropped out of both groups it would be tempting to conclude that the dropout affected the groups equally and that we can confidently conclude that the hard program was better. But this may not be an accurate conclusion. The reason is that workers in the two groups may have dropped out for *different* reasons, leaving behind two groups that are no longer comparable.

Consider this. What if the *least motivated* workers dropped out of the hard program (they felt it was too much work)? But the *most motivated* dropped out of the easy program (they felt unstimulated). (Figure 5.2 summarizes these events.) The end result would be that the workers left in the hard group were the most motivated, and the workers left in the easy group were the least motivated. If this were true, then the workers

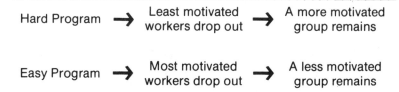

Figure 5.2 An Illustration of the Effects of Dropout on Comparison Groups

who received the hard program would have been more successful than those in the easy program, even if the two programs did not differ in effectiveness.

In any design in which there are comparison groups, and in which one of the groups is asked to participate to a greater degree, subjects may drop out of that group in response to the demands placed on them. This is a serious mortality problem because remaining subjects are likely to be more motivated and therefore more successful, on the average, than subjects in the other groups, where there has been less dropout. This situation is not uncommon in studies that attempt to show that some treatment or training program is successful.

One solution is to ensure that control groups (those that are used as a comparison so that we can show that the treated group did better) are as similar as possible to the treated group in terms of the time and effort required. For example, in the job training study above, workers in our control group may also be required to come to class. They may be asked to spend the same number of hours in class and to expend an effort similar to those in the treatment group. The only difference between the two groups would then be in the *content* of the training. Then, any subsequent difference in employment rates between the two groups will be due to the specific content of the training.

EXTERNAL VALIDITY

As we said earlier, internal validity factors represent plausible alternative hypotheses that the observed effect was due to some factor other than the experimental treatment or independent variable. To the extent that we can rule out these factors we can say that our study has internal validity: In this particular instance, with these subjects, the observed effect was due to the experimental treatment.

When we begin to talk about the generalizability of our findings to other settings, individuals, independent variables, and dependent variables, we are talking about external validity. Just as it was our goal to rule out factors of internal validity as alternative hypotheses, it is also our goal to rule out factors of external validity, in order that we may be able to generalize our findings. There are four such factors of external validity.

The first factor of external validity is the *interaction of testing and X* (also called the reactive effect of testing). This factor is a problem when taking a pretest *changes* the way a subject responds to the independent variable. Sometimes this is referred to as the "sensitizing effect" of a test. An example of a sensitizing test might be a questionnaire to measure prejudice, administered before and after a human relations training course. The items on the questionnaire may stimulate subjects to think about issues that they have not before considered: What are their attitudes toward minorities? Do they feel that minorities are different from nonminorities, and in what ways? Are their feelings and attitudes appropriate? Are they racist?

Given the very provocative nature of a questionnaire on prejudice, it is not surprising that a pretested subject's response to human relations training may be different from that of a subject who has not been tested. If there is a decrease in prejudice after the training we cannot be sure it was the training alone that was responsible for this change. If the pretest is in fact reactive, this may mean that only the combination of a sensitizing pretest followed by the training, resulted in decreased prejudice. In other words, it may be that the training "works" only when preceded by a pretest.

The interaction of testing and X is a concern only when the testing is unexpected, unusual, or causes subjects to change their behavior or thinking in some way. In some settings, such as school systems, tests are so common that they are an expected part of the environment, and are not likely to be sensitizing. In other words, there is usually little problem in using pretests in school settings. All other things being equal, the reactions of pretested students in one school system are likely to be indicative of the responses of students in other school systems, because testing is a common feature in all school settings. This supposes, of course, that the testing is of the type normally done in the schools. A highly unusual test may in fact sensitize student so that their reaction to a subsequent treatment or program is changed.

The interaction of testing and X can also be illustrated by looking at a study to evaluate the effectiveness of a weight loss program. The study used the following design:

Group A	R	O	X_1	O
Group B	R	O	X_0	O
Group C	R		X_1	O
Group D	R		X_0	O

To evaluate the effectiveness of the program in helping clients to lose weight, individuals were randomly assigned to four comparison groups. Two of the groups participated in the weight loss program that taught skills such as monitoring, stimulus control, shaping, and breaking chains of behavior. Exposure to this program is indicated by "X_1." The other two groups participated in group sessions of equal duration, but they did not receive training in any specific weight reduction procedures. These groups served as a control. Exposure to the control condition is indicated by "X_0."

In this design two of the groups were pretested and two were not. We chose this design because it allows us to illustrate the effects of a sensitizing pretest. What might a sensitizing pretest look like?

Let's suppose that a highly sensitizing pretest was used in this study: At the start of the first class session each subject was asked to come to the front of the room and to step on a scale. The subject's weight was then called off in front of the group and recorded on the researcher's data sheet. Given the embarrassment that most overweight people feel about their condition, it is not surprising that this pretest would change the way subjects respond to a weight loss program! In fact, peer pressure may be a strong motivator to work on weight reduction.

Figure 5.3 illustrates the outcome of our study, assuming that the weight loss program only worked for those subjects who were subjected to the embarrassing pretest. Note that the only one of the four groups to show a weight loss was the group that received the weight loss program *and* was pretested.

Another factor of external validity is the *interaction of selection and X*. We say that there is an interaction of selection and X when our results are applicable only to the particular persons and the particular situation that we have studied. If we cannot generalize our findings to different persons, locations, independent and dependent variables, then we have an interaction of selection and X. It should be obvious that we can

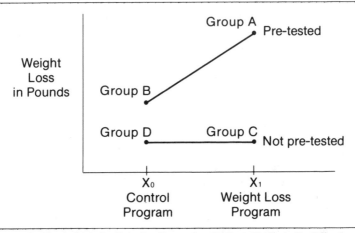

Figure 5.3   Illustration of a Reactive Pretest in a Study to Evaluate the Effectiveness of a Weight Reduction Training Program

almost never say that this factor is completely controlled. The extent to which we can generalize beyond the particulars of our study is partly a matter of judgment, and partly a matter of collecting additional data from other settings, persons, and so on. However, a reasonable goal might be to conduct our study so that the findings are generalizable to the greatest extent possible.

The interaction of selection and X is often a problem in demonstration studies. In this type of study, a group of researchers or planners gets a grant from a governmental or private source to set up a program that will "demonstrate" the effectiveness of a particular idea or service. For instance, a county public health department might set up a program of decentralized well-baby clinics as a demonstration of the effectiveness of accessible low-cost health services in reducing infant mortality in a particular area.

A problem often arises in that the researchers or planners have a vested interest in showing that their program works. So it is not uncommon for them to select demonstration sites that offer the best conditions for their program. For example, our county health department may set up their demonstration program in an area that has good public transportation, maximizing the likelihood that the well-baby clinics will be used. The limitation of this approach is that, while funders may be impressed with the results of the demonstration project, when the program is later applied to other areas or situations it does not work as well. If that is true, then what we have is clearly an interaction of selection and X: The result obtained in the demonstration project cannot necessarily be generalized to other settings.

Let's look at another example where we can again graphically illustrate the interaction of selection and X. Suppose that Dr. Feelgood, an internationally renowned therapist, has developed a Goal Setting Form (GSF). With the help of the GSF, the worker and client mutually agree upon goals to be worked on in therapy. Dr. Feelgood claims that use of this form with clients will result in higher client satisfaction. Since Dr. Feelgood holds an exclusive distributorship and copyright for the GSF, he is understandably eager to get mental health centers across the country to use the GSF. But in order to do that he must conduct research to substantiate his hypothesis. He decides to use the following research design:

$$R \qquad X_{GS} \qquad O$$
$$R \qquad \qquad \quad O$$

In this design one group of therapists uses the GSF with their clients and another group does not. At the conclusion of therapy all clients fill out a questionnaire indicating their level of satisfaction with the services received. Dr. Feelgood predicts with great confidence that the clients who received the GSF will report higher levels of satisfaction.

Dr. Feelgood runs into a bit of a hitch. It seems that some of the agencies in town are not as excited as Dr. F. about the potential benefits of the GSF. (It also turns out that the directors of some of the older agencies remember that unfortunate scandal some years back in which Dr. Feelgood was charged with running bogus sex therapy-assertion training groups.) At any rate, as luck will have it, the first five agencies approached by Dr. Feelgood as sites for his research project turn him down. "We've already got enough paperwork!" they say. Dr. Feelgood dismisses these agencies as organizations that are not open to innovation. Finally, he finds an agency that is very eager to cooperate. He carries out the study diagrammed above and confirms his hypothesis: Clients who receive the GSF are in fact more satisfied.

At this point we should be suspicious of Dr. Feelgood's claims. He did show that the GSF increased client satisfaction, but that was true in only one agency. We know that agencies that cooperate with researchers are different from those that do not: They are likely to have staff who are more open to new ideas, and more concerned about quality of service.

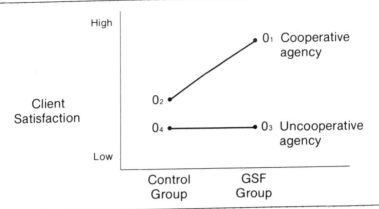

Figure 5.4 Illustration of the Interaction of Selection and X: A Program Works Only in a Cooperative Agency

We know further, that an interaction of selection and X is likely here. The GSF might not work in agencies that do not share these characteristics.

To illustrate the effect of an interaction of selection and X we will have to imagine that we are able to replicate, that is, to repeat, the study in one of the uncooperative agencies. The design would look like this:

Cooperative Agency	R	X_{GS}	O_1
	R		O_2
	R	X_{GS}	O_3
Uncooperative Agency	R		O_4

Figure 5.4 is a graph in which the four group's average posttest satisfaction scores are plotted. This illustrates an interaction of selection and X because it shows that the GSF results in high client satisfaction only when used in a cooperative agency. In an uncooperative agency, where workers are perhaps less open to innovation, and less concerned with the quality of service, the GSF appears to have no impact at all. In this case, as in other situations in which there is an interaction of selection and X, we cannot necessarily generalize our findings to other settings.

Another threat to external validity is called *reactive arrangements*. Reactive arrangements become a concern when the setting of the study is artificial or different in some way from what would routinely be expected in that setting. Reactive arrangements limit generalizability of findings to the extent that the effects observed in the study would not occur in the real world, outside of the experimental situation.

In the 1930s a group of industrial researchers conducted a series of studies directed at improving the productivity of workers in the General Electric plant in Hawthorne. The unexpected findings of these studies have been classic examples of effects due to reactive arrangements. In fact, this phenomenon is sometimes referred to as the "Hawthorne effect." (Homans, 1965).

In the Hawthorne studies a group of researchers in their white lab coats descended upon the plant and proceeded to carry out a number of experiments that were highly visible to the workers in the plant. In one of these studies, the researchers examined the effect of various changes in work conditions on the speed with which workers produced wire relay boards. They tried altering the size of the work group, lowering and raising the level of illumination in the work area, changing the size of the room, and so on.

To their surprise the Hawthorne researchers found that *any* change resulted in an increased output of relay boards. Even when the room lighting was lowered to a level that made it difficult to see how to solder the wires, output still went up. What had happened?

The researchers in this study failed to realize that they had created an artificial situation. The workers who were selected for study were aware of the study and of the fact that they were being closely monitored. They were probably flattered by the attention they received. The most likely explanation for their curious behavior is that the artificial nature of the situation prompted the workers to try to play the role of a good subject. They tried to figure out what the researchers expected of them—in this case it was increased productivity—and they acted accordingly. The problem of course was that the responses of these workers to the various changes in work conditions were not typical: They could not be generalized to other plants that were not being studied.

Reactive arrangements are likely to threaten the external validity of any study in which the subjects are placed in new or unusual situations, that is, situations that are not typical of the real world to which we would like to generalize our results. That sometimes happens in schools when a new program is introduced and creates an unusual situation, like a lot of excitement on the part of teachers, a change in routine, or a new way to group students. In the laboratory experiments that are so often obligatory for undergraduate psychology students, reactive arrangements should always be taken account of. They are less likely to limit the generalizability of studies of motor reaction time or color perception. But the laboratory behavior of a student who is asked to problem solve, to cooperate with others, or to state an opinion, may be very different from the behavior of that student in the real world.

A final threat to external validity occurs when several treatments or interventions are administered in sequence to the same persons. The researcher's concern here is that the effects of prior interventions cannot be erased. Consider, for instance, a study to determine whether punishment or praise is more effective in getting emotionally disturbed children to comply with requests from a teacher. During an initial period the child is punished for lack of compliance; during a later period the punishment is dropped but the teacher provides praise whenever the child complies. The level of compliance is monitored throughout— perhaps by recording the proportion of teacher requests that are obeyed. The design looks like this:

$$O_1 \qquad X_{punish} \qquad O_2 \qquad X_{praise} \qquad O_3 \qquad O_4$$

If the children's compliance increases at O_3 and O_4 we cannot say with confidence that this change was the result of praise. It may have been the result of the punishment: Perhaps it just took a while for the punishment to set in, a delayed effect. Or, it may be that praise alone is not effective. Only when praise follows punishment is the contrast and relief great enough to make that praise effective in increasing compliance.

When there are more than two treatments—such as in a study to evaluate the effectiveness of five different drugs—it is even more difficult to determine which single intervention or combination or sequence of interventions is responsible for any observed changes. (In Chapter 6 we will learn how to use a different type of research design to evaluate the effects of multiple treatments.)

GROUP RESEARCH DESIGNS

Now that we understand the factors that pose threats to the internal and external validity of research designs, let us look at some common group designs.

(1) The One Shot Case Study   X O

This is the most rudimentary of the designs. In this design a single individual, family, group, community, or other unit is studied at one point in time, to determine the effect of some treatment or other independent variable. Campbell and Stanley (1963) argue that use of this design is hardly ever justified because it provides a total lack of control for all of the threats to internal and external validity that we have discussed.

For example, this design has been used to study the behavior of an autistic child. The purpose was to discover the effects of autism on the full range of child behaviors. But in this study it would be impossible to determine if any observed behavior was a result of autism or whether it was specific to this particular child. For example, some aspects of the child's current behavior may be due to history, say a medical emergency that occurred during the course of the child's development. We have no way of knowing if this child's behavior is typical of autistic behavior in other children, and hence there is no control for the interaction of selection and X.

The situation may be improved somewhat by studying several, rather than one, child. We might even counter the effects of an interaction of selection and X by randomly choosing our autistic children from some defined population of such children. But even so, this design leaves most factors of internal validity uncontrolled.

Campbell and Stanley (1963) note that the weakness of this design is that it fails to provide comparison. We have no point of reference. Since we study the unit or sample at only one point in time we cannot compare an observation or test with subsequent tests. And there is no comparison group to serve as a benchmark. In this example, it would be impossible to identify the effects of autism unless we could compare the behavior of our subject or subjects to the behavior of normal children.

Campbell and Stanley note further, that in one shot case studies, a great deal of effort is often put into studying the single case intensively. Since this design provides virtually no conclusive evidence about the effects of X, they suggest that this effort would be better used in studying fewer details, and in putting the effort saved into formation of a comparison group.

(2) The One Group Pretest
Posttest Design O_1 X O_2

This design represents an improvement over Design 1 because it provides at least a minimal point of comparison: The researcher can look at the difference in performance between the pretest and the posttest. Because this design is easy to implement—it does not require the recruitment and testing of a control group—it is often used. But it is a weak design because, like Design 1, it fails to rule out most of the threats to internal and external validity.

For example, assume that we used Design 2 to evaluate the job training program discussed earlier in this chapter. (That is, "X" represents a job training program and the "Os" represent measures of the number of days of employment during specific periods.) From that discussion it should be easy to see that any change in employment rates between O_1 and O_2 may be due to a number of factors other than the training program itself. For example, they may be due to an improvement in the economy during the course of the study (history) or to the particular individuals selected for the program, who may not be typical of unemployed workers (interaction of selection and X).

There is another type of history (a factor of internal validity) that we have not discussed, but which is likely, in some situations, to affect the results in a study using this design. These are effects of history due to *season* and *institutional event schedules*.

For example, imagine that you are director of the Student Counseling Center at Big Shot University. Big Shot University is a great place to be, but it is very competitive, so competitive, in fact, that many students are becoming ill due to stress. You decide it's time to do something about the problem. You select a group of students to participate in a series of stress management workshops over a period of several weeks. A stress questionnaire is used to assess their level of stress before and after the program. To your dismay, you find that the level of stress has actually increased after the workshops.

Your program may have been a victim of institutional event schedule. Since the stress workshops took several weeks to carry out, it was necessary to pretest the students at the beginning of the semester. The posttest took place toward the end of the semester. As luck would have it, that happened to be the period immediately before final exams! The increase in stress may have been due to this factor, so it is impossible to make any conclusion about the effectiveness of the stress management workshops on the level of student stress.

Seasonal events can also wreck havoc with Design 2. For instance, a study to evaluate the effectiveness of a program to treat depression will have to take account of anticipated variations in mood that are associated with the weather: In northern climates people tend to be more depressed during the long gray winter months.

Maturation, instrumentation, and regression may also present problems in interpreting the results of Design 2: There may be changes over time independent of X that affect the dependent variable, the calibration of the measuring instrument may change, or the subjects in the study may have been selected because of their extreme scores. The fact that subjects were pretested may also affect their performance on the posttest even if X had no effect. As we will see later, these weaknesses are inherent in any design that does not use a comparison group. When we include a comparison group in our design we can distribute many of these internal validity factors equally between the groups. Then, any difference between the groups must be due to X rather than to these factors.

One way in which this design differs from the one shot case study is that this design employs a pretest. Therefore the two factors of testing (internal validity) and the interaction of testing and X (external validity) may be of concern. For example, if "X" is a reading improvement program and the "Os" represent administration of reading tests, we would expect some improvement on the posttest even if the program had no effect. That improvement would be the result of having had some practice in taking the test earlier. This design does not allow us to separate out any improvement due to the program from the effects of testing. This makes it difficult to interpret the findings.

An interaction of testing and X is of concern if the testing is novel or unusual. Suppose that we used Design 2 to evaluate the effect of a teacher training program on the classroom performance of high school teachers. A common method for judging teacher performance is to have the school principal or some other important person observe a class session. The "Os" in our design may represent such an observation. But as any high school student can tell us, who has seen his or her teacher develop a sudden burst of motivation on classroom observation day, classroom observation is a reactive measurement. The teacher's performance under observation may not be typical of that teacher's day to day class performance. Therefore, any effects of our training program may not apply beyond the observation days.

(3) The Static Group Comparison   X O_1

O_2

In this design, a group that has experienced "X" is compared to one that has not. The two groups may be already formed (such as two classrooms) or they may be self-selected groups (such as voters and nonvoters). The static group comparison represents a substantial improvement over the first two designs because of the introduction of a comparison group. There is now a benchmark (control group) against which to compare the performance of the experimental group.

The factor of internal validity that is of greatest concern in this design is selection. Remember, the groups in this design are not formed by random assignment, a procedure that tends to distribute all subject characteristics equally between comparison groups. Where we have groups that were not formed by random assignment we cannot be sure that the groups were truly equivalent. This is a problem because any difference between O_1 and O_2 cannot be attributed solely to "X"; it may be due to the fact that the two groups differed in ways that affected the dependent variable.

Imagine that "X" is a program to improve the math skills of third graders. In this design the program is run in Classroom A while Classroom B serves as a control. The problem is that a difference in math performance between the two classes may be due to differences between the classes—for example, the children in Classroom A may be brighter, or the teacher may be more enthusiastic about the program. Any difference in math performance between the two groups may be due to these selection differences, to the program, or to a combination of the two.

Mortality can be another serious limitation of this design. In many studies, subjects who receive the "X" are called upon to make a greater effort than those in the control group—for example, they may have to participate in a training program that requires a lot of work. In such situations, the least motivated subjects will tend to drop out of the experimental group, leaving behind an experimental group that is more highly motivated, on average, than the control group. In our discussion of the job training program above, we saw how this causes a bias in favor of finding that the program was successful, even if it was not.

The absence of pretests in this design has advantages and disadvantages. A disadvantage is that without pretests we have no check as to whether the groups are really similar on the dependent variable. If we measure IQ level after some intervention, it would be nice to know that the pretest IQ levels of the two groups were similar. If they were, we could have more confidence in our findings. It is not always possible, however, to include a pretest. The data may not be available or we may not have the time or money to do more than one testing. In some situations it makes no sense to do a pretest. This was true in Dr. Feelgood's study on client satisfaction with services (Figure 5.4). The client satisfaction measure could only be given after the client received the service that was being evaluated.

An advantage of not pretesting is that the interaction of testing and X is ruled out as a source of bias in the design. If the testing process is reactive (such as our classroom observations) then the absence of pretests allows us to generalize our findings to groups that are not normally pretested.

(4) The Nonequivalent Control Group Design   O   X   O

                                               O   O

This design is equivalent to the static group comparison, with the addition of pretests. The inclusion of a comparison group that is evaluated at the same time as the experimental group, adds to the strength of the design. The two groups in Design 4 may be already formed groups, such as two school classrooms. Or the groups may be self-selected. For example, the experimental group may be composed of subjects who sought the services of an agency, and the control group may be selected from among those who did not seek services.

It is important to remember that the groups in this design are not formed by random assignment. This means that we still cannot rule out the possibility that important differences exist between the groups that might affect the results. However, in this design we have at least a rough estimate of comparability in that we are able to compare pretest performance of the two groups.

In group designs in which we use pretests it is customary to run statistical tests between the groups to see if they differ on the dependent variable (say, some measure of performance) and on other variables that might that affect the dependent variable (say, sex, race, or income). As long as these tests indicate no significant differences, we have some assurance that the groups were equivalent. Nevertheless, it is important to be vigilant for differences between the groups that may influence the results. For example, as we saw earlier, if volunteers are recruited for the experimental group and nonvolunteers for the control group, this selection factor may invalidate the results.

A better method for achieving equivalent comparison groups is, of course, to form these groups through random assignment. But this is often impossible. For example, if we want to study differences between men and women, or between blue-collar workers and white-collar workers, we are not able to assign individuals to one or the other of these groups. (For this reason Design 4 is a nonexperimental design.) In such situations, Design 4 is an excellent alternative to an experimental design using groups formed by random assignment.

Because we have a simultaneous comparison in this design, most of the sources of internal validity are ruled out as possible explanations for our findings. It is possible, but unlikely, that effects of maturation, history, testing, or instrumentation would be a problem. This is because any effect of these factors in one group is likely to be equivalent in the other group. For example, if pretesting leads subjects to do a bit better on the posttest, this will be equally true for subjects in both groups. Any difference between the groups, then, cannot be attributed to having taken a pretest. In other words, control group designs *control* for factors of internal validity.

We should, however, note one type of history that may not be controlled, even when we have a comparison group. This factor is called *intrasession history*. It refers to any event that occurs in one group but not in the other. For example, in our stress management training study at Big Shot University, one of the groups could have been exposed (inadvertently) to a fire drill during the training or the testing. This factor of intrasession history represents a way in which the comparison groups differed (assuming that the control subjects were in another building and did not experience the fire drill). In general it should be possible to at least monitor such instances. It is also important to make every effort to expose comparison groups to conditions that are as similar as possible, with the exception of the treatment or independent variable.

Regression may be a problem in a design with two comparison groups, but only if one group is selected because of its extreme scores. So, for example, if we study the effect of a training program on low-achievement children compared to average achievers, we should expect that at least part of the improvement of the low achievers on the posttest will be due to regression. To avoid this problem it is best to use one of the experimental designs described below. In these designs, comparison groups are formed by random assignment so that extreme scorers, and hence regression effects, are distributed equally between the groups. Any difference between the groups, then, could not be due to regression.

(5), (6), and (7) True Experimental Designs

(5)	R	O	X	O	Pretest Posttest Control
	R	O		O	Group Design
(6)	R	O	X	O	Solomon Four Group
	R	O		O	Design
	R		X	O	
	R			O	
(7)	R		X	O	Posttest Only Control
	R			O	Group Design

The defining characteristic of these designs is that they all use groups formed by random assignment. As we have said before, this is the best way to ensure that comparison groups are equivalent, although it is not a guarantee. When using Design 5 the researchers should compare the pretest scores of the groups as an additional check. In any situation in which comparison groups are used, the researcher can also compare the groups on any demographic variables for which he or she has data: sex, age, race, and so on. The results of the study must be tempered by any differences found between the groups.

All three of these designs generally control for all factors of internal validity. This is a result of using groups formed by random assignment, and of ensuring that the groups are equivalent in all ways except for exposure to the independent variable in the experimental groups. In this situation any factor of internal validity that is operative affects the comparison groups equally. Therefore, any difference between the groups cannot be due to these factors.

We should pause for a moment to consider the meaning of the phrase "experimental designs control for factors of internal validity." By this we do not mean that these factors are magically erased. For example, in our study of birth control, we have no way to eliminate events of history, such as an economic depression or a new law that makes it difficult to obtain contraceptives over the counter. What we *can* do is to use an experimental design that distributes the impact of these factors equally over the comparison groups. Then any observed difference between groups cannot be due to these factors. We say they are controlled. What we have done is to rule out plausible alternative hypotheses—hypotheses alternative to the experimental hypothesis.(The experimental hypothesis, you will remember, is that the treatment or independent variable is responsible for the observed difference.)

Despite the excellent control that these designs provide for internal validity, we cannot blindly assume that all factors are controlled each time we use one of these designs. For example, intrasession history may not be controlled if one, but not another, group is exposed to an event such as a fire drill or an accident.

If subjects drop out of our study we may also have a mortality problem. As we said earlier this may be a problem even if equal numbers of persons drop out of each group, because dropout may occur for different reasons in different groups. Then, the groups that remain may be different in important ways. Since dropout is a common problem in research studies, it is useful to suggest solutions to this problem.

Campbell and Stanley (1963) suggest that if subjects drop out of the treatment, the researcher should still use the data of all subjects (including the dropouts) on both the pretest and the posttest. This will bias the results in a conservative direction: That is, by "weakening" the effect of the treatment, you will make it less likely that the results will show that the treatment had its intended effect. If, despite this conservative bias, your data show that the treatment worked, you can be confident of the validity of that finding.

This is certainly a valid solution. However, in the experience of the authors, when subjects drop out of a treatment or intervention, they are rarely available to take the posttest. We are left with the problem of missing data. There are statistical procedures available to handle missing data problems. Perhaps the most common is the "replacement with means" method. In this method, each missing score is replaced by the average score on that variable for all available scores. In other words, the researcher makes the assumption that each person who was not measured would have gotten an average score had he or she stuck around to be measured.

However, this is not a good solution because we may not be justified in assuming that the dropouts were "average." There are statistical problems as well, which are beyond the scope of this book. There really is no good after-the-fact solution to the problem of missing data. There are, however, ways to *prevent* the problem. As in so many other endeavors, prevention is the best solution.

If the study requires attendance at treatment and testing sessions, we can provide incentives for subjects to show up. The senior author was part of a research and training team involved in evaluating interpersonal skill development groups. We required a cash deposit from each person who signed up to participate in our six-week group sessions. A certain portion was refunded if the subject attended the treatment sessions, with a larger amount refunded if all sessions were attended. Additional portions of the deposit were refunded for participating in the posttest assessment (immediately following treatment) and in the follow-up assessment (three to six months after training). The subject could regain the entire deposit by attending all treatment and evaluation sessions. In addition, we made each session attractive to participants by providing comfortable furnishings and refreshments.

In longitudinal studies, in which subjects must be followed and measured over a long period of time, mortality is a particularly crucial issue. Marriage and change of name, change of phone numbers, and moving often make it difficult to locate subjects. A common procedure to help in locating subjects is to ask them at the beginning of the study to provide the names, addresses, and phone numbers of two adults who are likely to know where they can be reached.

Another important issue in designs involving more than one group concerns the events occurring in the control group. In our notation a blank space appears in the control groups during the time when the experimental groups are experiencing the "X." This is a bit misleading. As we have seen, it is important that comparison groups be as similar as possible with the exception of the treatment or independent variable. So, if we want to know if the specific content of our experimental treatment leads to the desired change, we must make sure that the control subjects receive a control "treatment" that takes as much effort and arouses as much expectation of improvement as the experimental treatment. Then any difference between groups must be due to the specific treatment and not to the fact that experimental subjects worked hard, that they expected to change, or that they merely had contact with a helper.

This is why medical researchers use a sugar placebo when evaluating the effectiveness of a drug. The effectiveness of any drug may be due to the fact that the patient receiving it believed that it worked. When we give a placebo drug to subjects in the control group we are controlling for the expectancy effect. We compare the result in the experimental group (patients who received the real drug) to the result in the control group (patients who received the sugar pill). Assuming the drug worked, the difference represents the effectiveness of the drug above and beyond that due to the mere fact of expecting to benefit, or attention from a doctor.

The point of all this is to remind you that while our notation makes it appear that nothing is happening to control group subjects during the treatment period, that is never the case. In our experiments it is important to control for attention and effort by providing control subjects with an experience comparable to experimental subjects—with the exception of the treatment itself.

For example, suppose you wanted to study the effectiveness of a film in reducing prejudice. You could use Design 5. Using a questionnaire you would measure level of prejudice before and after the film. The experimental subjects would of course see the antiprejudice film. The control subjects should be exposed to a similar experience without the specific antiprejudice content. We need to control for the effect that seeing a film—any film—might have on responses to the questionnaire. So, while the experimental subjects are seeing the antiprejudice film, control subjects would be viewing a film of approximately equal length, on a neutral topic, not related to prejudice.

Another example of the use of an appropriate control group comes from a study conducted by the Benjamin Rose Institute in Cleveland in the mid-1960s. These researchers developed an intensive casework program designed to improve or maintain the functioning of frail elderly people who were no longer competent to care for themselves (Blenkner et al., 1971).

Using Design 5, they randomly assigned clients to two groups: The experimental group received the intensive casework program that included counseling, financial assistance, guardianship, and a number of other interventions. In deciding how to deal with the control group the researchers realized that it would be unfair to compare their program to no services at all. Many of the frail elderly receive at least some services—perhaps a visiting nurse or some financial assistance. So, in order to show that their program worked, they knew they had to compare it to what was normally available to the frail elderly in that community. So, in the control group, clients continued to receive the services that they would normally have received had they not been selected for study.

(As it turned out, the intensive casework program did not lead to much improvement over and beyond what clients could expect as the result of receiving regular services. Had the researchers used an artificially constructed control group in which no services were provided, we might have been led to conclude incorrectly that the intensive program had an effect, when it did not. See the Case Study following this chapter.)

So far we have discussed the internal validity of the three true experimental designs. What about their external validity? To the extent that the subjects in any of these designs are not typical of the population to which we want to generalize our findings, the interaction of selection and X is not controlled. Controlling for this factor is dependent on obtaining a representative sample. To the extent that a study using one of these designs creates an atypical situation that makes subjects respond to the treatment in a way that they would not, if they were not being studied, reactive arrangements are not controlled. The solution is to study the effect of your treatment in as naturalistic a setting as possible.

Design 5 is the only one of the three designs that will fail to control for the interaction of testing and X when the pretest is sensitizing, that is, when it changes the way subjects respond to the treatment or independent variable. If our testing procedure is sensitizing, and we would like to generalize our findings to the world at large (where pretests are not used), then Designs 6 and 7 are preferable.

Let us return, for example, to our evaluation of the teacher training program, in which we measure the teacher's classroom performance by sending the principal in to observe the teacher's instruction. We want to evaluate how effective our program is in producing better teachers, without having to limit our conclusions to situations in which teachers are evaluated in this manner. Does the training program work even if we don't send the principal in to observe?

Although Design 7 looks sparse it is actually a powerful design. It uses comparison groups formed by random assignment and it resolves the problem of sensitizing pretests by avoiding them. However, this design should be used only where there can be some assurance that the comparison groups are equivalent. If the experimental and control groups of teachers differ in level of competence, enthusiasm, or years of experience, it will not be clear whether our results are due to these factors, to our program, or to their combination.

Design 6, the Solomon four-group design, might be used in its place. Not only does this design control for the interaction of testing and X, it actually allows us to measure the influence, if any, of the pretest on the results. We do this by comparing the results for the pretested (first two) groups, with the results for the unpretested (second two) groups. This design is actually a combination of Designs 5 and 7, so it enables us to repeat or replicate our finding: Any difference in performance as a result of our treatment should be evident in the difference between the first two groups, and in the difference between the second two groups.

A disadvantage of this design is that since it uses four groups, it requires a greater number of subjects. If a limited number of subjects is available, we may want to devise a less sensitizing test so that we can use Design 5, the pretest posttest control group design. For example, where student evaluations are routinely used, we may want to measure teacher performance in this way, rather than by sending the school principal in for a classroom observation. Of course, when our testing procedure is not likely to be sensitizing, Design 5 is the design of choice.

SUMMARY

Research designs are plans. They specify the sequencing and arrangement of independent and dependent variables in our research studies. The purpose of research design is to help us establish that an independent variable or variables, or a treatment, is responsible for some observed effect, such as client improvement. This is the experimental hypothesis.

Research designs are helpful in that they assist us in eliminating plausible alternative hypotheses, that is, hypotheses that factors other than the independent variable or treatment are responsible for the observed effect. These factors fall into two categories: those associated with internal, and those associated with external validity.

Internal validity issues concern the extent to which we can conclude that our treatment or independent variable was indeed responsible for the observed effect in our study: for the subjects, settings, and independent variables employed in this particular instance. External validity concerns the extent to which the observed findings can be generalized to other subjects, settings, treatments, and measures. A number of research designs, varying in their ability to control for factors of internal and external validity, are available for the researcher's use.

CASE STUDY

A Group Research Design

Blenkner, M., Bloom, M., & Nielsen, M. (1971, October). A research and demonstration project of protective services. *Social Casework,* *52*(8), 483-499.

This was one of the earliest human service research studies to use an experimental design. Even today, two decades later, it stands as an example of a carefully designed and well-controlled research study. It became somewhat infamous because of a surprising and disturbing finding that we will present at the end of this case study.

The research was conducted in the mid-1960s in Cleveland, Ohio. It was sponsored by the Benjamin Rose Institute, a large and well-known agency that serves the elderly. Margaret Blenkner and her colleagues had become aware of a critical problem among the elderly living in the community. Human service workers had been finding an increasing number of very old persons who were no longer able to care for themselves, but had no one else to help. Some of these older people suffered from physical disabilities that hampered their ability to prepare food, to groom, and to do other tasks of daily living. Others were mentally incompetent. Their disorientation or confusion made them a danger to themselves and sometimes to others.

The Benjamin Rose Institute believed that a program of intensive casework services could benefit these older persons, whom they called elderly protectives. So they designed such a program and set out to demonstrate its usefulness. To do that they chose to use a variation of Design 5, the pretest, posttest control group design. By comparing elderly protectives who received the intensive service with those who did not, they hoped to show that their program was helpful to the elderly.

The researchers decided to include in their sample elderly protectives who were referred to the Benjamin Rose Institute by one of thirteen community agencies. In a typical case, an elderly protective would come to the attention of the Visiting Nurse Association or the Public Aid department, and these agencies contacted the Institute for help. Over a twelve-month period from June 1964 to May 1965, 164 elderly protectives were recruited. As each case folder came into the Institute, it was randomly assigned to one of two groups. Protectives in the Service (Experimental) group received a specially designed program of intensive services for a period of one year from their referral. Those assigned to the Control group continued to receive only those services normally available in the community.

Both groups were carefully evaluated at the time of referral and again one year later. The researchers conducted intensive interviews with protectives and their collaterals. (A collateral was defined as the person most closely involved with the protective, usually a friend, relative, or neighbor.) They interviewed staff members of the agencies that had referred the protective. They observed and rated the quality of the protective's physical environment, such as the adequacy of housing. They administered Mental Status tests to protectives to determine their orientation and judgment. And finally, they kept track of how long each protective lived (this variable was called Survival) and whether the protective was placed in an institution (Institutionalization). On these last two variables the researchers followed up for seven years to see which protectives had survived and which had been institutionalized.

The design can be summarized as follows:

```
R   O   X   O   O   O   O   O   O   O      Service Group
R   O       O   O   O   O   O   O   O      Control Group
```

This design illustrates an issue we discussed in Chapter 6. While the notation makes it appear that nothing was happening to protectives in the control group during the demonstration year, that was clearly not the case. As we said, Control participants continued to receive the services that were normally available to them. And after the demonstration year, the Service protectives no longer received the intensive casework program. In other words, after the first year, both groups continued to receive some services. Didn't this make it difficult to show that the Service program worked?

The answer is yes. But that wasn't necessarily a bad thing. It would certainly have been easier to show that the intensive Service program worked if we compared it to a control group of elderly protectives who received no services whatsoever. But that really would not have been possible for ethical reasons. All of the protectives were in critical, life-threatening situations and had to be helped. It would not have been possible or ethical to ask the referring agencies to withdraw their services.

But there is another reason why using a control group that received some services is a good idea. It decreases the likelihood that our design will be limited by the interaction of selection and X. Remember, interaction of selection and X is a problem where the results cannot be generalized beyond the particular events in our study. If we want to know if our program works in the real world, we need to use a real world comparison in our design. It was more realistic to compare an intensive Service program to a Control program of limited services, because in the real world, many frail elderly do receive at least limited services. Comparison with a totally unserved Control group would have stacked the cards in the researchers' favor. It would leave open the possibility that even if our study found the program worked, that it might not be an improvement over what was already available in the community.

As it turned out, the Service program did not work as well as the Benjamin Rose Institute had hoped. Although protectives in the Service group did better in a couple of ways (for instance, their collaterals reported significantly less stress as a result of the program), for the most part the two groups did not differ. However, there were two very troubling differences. At every point over the seven-year follow-up, protectives in the Service group were more likely to find themselves in a nursing home. More troubling still, they had a consistent pattern of early death. Those who received the intensive services died sooner than those who did not.

Because it includes a pretest, one of the advantages of the pretest, posttest control group design is that it allows the researcher to see if the comparison groups were similar at the start of the study (at least on the variables for which data are available). As we said in Chapter 5, groups formed by random assignment, as they were in this study, tend to be very similar.

But this study illustrated that this is not always the case. In an attempt to understand the troubling finding of early death, the senior author and a colleague reanalyzed the Benjamin Rose data (Berger & Piliavin, 1976a, 1976b). They found that, on the average, Service participants were somewhat older than Control participants. It *is* possible that this difference contributed to the earlier death of Service participants.

It also appeared that the Service participants were more debilitated: They had lower physical functioning and mental status scores on the pretest. However, it was not clear if these two differences were real because a great deal of the pretest data on these variables were missing. Either they had not been collected or they were never recorded. As a result, the unhappy findings of this study remain clouded in mystery to this day.

NOTE

1. There is some disagreement in the literature as to whether longitudinal studies do indeed fail to show a decline in intelligence with age, which is apparent in cross-sectional studies. Botwinick (1978) argues that both types of research show a decline in intellectual abilities with age, although "longitudinal research tends to reflect lesser decline, starting later in life" (p. 225). Nevertheless, this example illustrates the importance of understanding research design.

Chapter 6

SINGLE SUBJECT RESEARCH DESIGNS

In the last chapter we discussed research involving groups of people. In this chapter we will be talking about research that focuses primarily upon one person, one group, or one unit. This type of research is often referred to as single subject research, single case research, "n of one" research, and research using time series designs.

Single subject research can be used to study direct services, planning, and administration, and it provides for immediate and practical feedback. It allows professionals to improve their practice and develop theories for intervention.

With single subject research we are concerned about two important questions:

(1) Was there a change in behavior?
(2) Was our intervention responsible for the change?

In order to answer these questions we must first be able to collect data about the behavior so that we can tell if it did in fact change. In social science research the methods available for data collection include interviews, questionnaires, standardized tests, such as the MMPI and the WAIS, records or archives, such as agency records or governmental documents, and direct observation.

Direct observation is a primary method of data collection in single subject research. Observations can be made by an independent observer or in some cases by the client, who serves the function of monitoring (observing) his or her own behavior.

STRATEGIES FOR
OBSERVATIONAL RECORDING

When observations of behavior are made, they must be recorded. Social scientists working in the area of social learning theory (i.e., behavior modification) have developed methods for recording observations, although these methods can be used by researchers in any discipline. These methods are frequency measures, interval recording, and duration measures.

Frequency measures. Observers using frequency measures record the number of times a behavior occurs in a given period of time. Frequency measures are the most common way to measure behavior. The number of cigarettes smoked, the number of swear words used by an adolescent, the number of times late for work, or the number of classes missed, are all frequency measures.

This method is especially appropriate when the observed behaviors are discrete, and can thus be counted with ease. In addition, the behavior should take place for a relatively constant amount of time each time it occurs.

Continuous behaviors are generally not suitable for frequency recording. These include ongoing behaviors such as smiling, sitting in one's seat, talking, lying down, and reading a book.

Duration measures. With duration measures, the length of time that a behavior occurs during an observation period is recorded. For example, the researcher can record the amount of time that junior high school students spend sitting in their seats during their study period. The researcher records the total amount of time that they are seated regardless of the number of times they leave their seat.

When recording the duration of a behavior, the observer can measure time in seconds or minutes by using a stopwatch, or by recording the time that the behavior begins and ends at each occurrence. Duration measures are particularly useful when the goal is to increase or decrease the length of time a response is performed. However, duration measures can be used only when the onset and termination of the behavior are clearly defined.

Interval recording. Interval recording measures the behavior in terms of units of time rather than discrete occurrences. Usually we take a single block of time such as a 30- or 60-minute time period each day. The block of time is divided into short intervals of 10, 20, 30, or more seconds. During each interval we observe a client's behavior. If the behavior occurs during that interval, a response is scored. This is true if the behavior occurs only once or many times during the interval.

This is the most flexible way to measure behavior. All we record is the presence or absence of a behavior in each interval. Thus interval recording is suitable for discrete behavior as well as ongoing behavior such as sitting in one's seat.

Interval recording can also be used to record duration. If a behavior occurs during the entire interval then it gets recorded. However, if the behavior occurs only during a portion of the interval, then it gets recorded as though it never occurred. For example, suppose we were interested in increasing the attention span of Mikey, a preschooler who pays very little attention to tasks being performed. During nursery school when it is time to color, work on stacking blocks, put puzzles together, or perform any other age-appropriate activities, Mikey does not watch what he is doing, but looks away.

We could divide the time spent on coloring, stacking blocks, and assembling puzzles into 10-second intervals. During these intervals we would record if Mikey's eyes were focused on the activity during the entire interval. On a recording sheet we could note whether Mikey was paying attention (eyes focused on the activity) or not paying attention (eyes not focused on the activity) for each 10-second interval. If he was focused on the activity for less than the entire 10 seconds, it would be recorded that he was not paying attention. This method gives us a good approximation of the total amount of time that Mikey was paying attention to play tasks.

ISSUES AND PROBLEMS
IN SAMPLING BEHAVIOR

The purpose of monitoring is to get a representative sample or accurate picture of how often or how long a behavior occurs. Often behavior fluctuates widely over a given day or week or month. Therefore, we must be careful not to allow these fluctuations to misrepresent the overall rate of occurrence. For instance, if a child's temper tantrums occur only in the presence of the child's mother, then we would monitor the behavior at times when mother was present. Otherwise, we would get a distorted picture of the child's behavior. In order to assess accurately the occurrence of behavior we must make the following decisions about monitoring.

(1) We must decide on the number of times data will be collected per day, week, or month. Our decision depends on how much the behavior varies. If the behavior is very stable from one day to the next, then daily assessment is less essential.

(2) The length of time to be set aside for the observation period must be determined. Behavior should be observed for a period of time that will yield data that are representative of typical performance.

(3) We must decide when the observations should be made. Do we conduct the observations in the morning, afternoon, or evening, during school hours, or on weekends? We can record behavior in a single block of time in a single day or at different times throughout the day. For instance, if a behavior occurs only during a specific time of day (e.g., lunch time), then this time of the day should be monitored. An advantage of observing behavior at various times throughout the day is that the observed behavior is more likely to be representative of the true occurrence.

(4) If interval recording is used, we must decide on the length of the interval. If the behavior occurs frequently, then short intervals should be used (e.g., 10-15 seconds). If long intervals are used with high-frequency behaviors, many behaviors will be counted as one occurrence and a change in the frequency of behavior might go undetected. Using very short intervals (5 seconds or less), however, it is very difficult for observers to score because the pace is too fast. If the behavior being measured is continuous (e.g., watching TV, reading) the length of the interval may not be as important as when the behavior is discrete, because longer or shorter intervals are not as likely to exclude "instances" of continuous behavior.

Estimating reliability. Behavior must be defined and measured carefully if an observer is going to be confident that the observations are accurate. In order to ensure that we are recording *consistently*, at some point we need to ask two independent observers to record the *same* behavior at the *same* time, using the *same* type of recording methods. We then compare their observations and hope they are similar. Specifically, we can compute the percentage of agreement between two observers. If the percentage of agreement is high (70% or higher), then there is high reliability (i.e., both observers agree most of the time).

For frequency measures we use the following formula to calculate the reliability:

$$\text{Percentage of Agreement} = \frac{\text{Lowest Frequency Observed}}{\text{Highest Frequency Observed}} \times 100\%$$

Let's look at an example to see how this formula works. In a preschool program there is a child named Tommy. Tommy is aggressive and will hit other children in his class. The teacher and the teacher's aide decide that they will record the frequency of Tommy's hitting other children during the next week of classes. They determine operational definitions of "hitting," and decide to record the frequencies. At the end of the week the teacher and the aide compare the data that they have recorded. The teacher recorded 15 instances of Tommy's hitting and the teacher's aide recorded 12 instances. The reliability of their observations is 80%. This was calculated using the above formula:

$$\text{Percentage Agreement} = \frac{12}{15} \times 100\% = 80\%$$

The number 80% is a relatively high percentage agreement, so we have some confidence that our recording is reliable.

For duration measures, the reliability is calculated by a similar formula:

$$\text{Percentage of Agreement} = \frac{\text{Lowest Duration Observed}}{\text{Highest Duration Observed}} \times 100\%$$

To calculate the reliability of interval recording we first have to define what we mean by an "agreement" and a "disagreement." If both observers record an occurrence of the behavior in the *same* interval, we have an agreement. If one observer does, and the other does not, then we have a disagreement. Now, knowing the difference between agreements and disagreements we can compute the reliability using the following formula:

Percentage of
Agreement   = $\dfrac{\text{Number of Agreements}}{\text{No. of Agreements + No. of Disagreements}} \times 100\%$

Note that intervals in which neither observer recorded a behavior are not included in the denominator of this formula.

Let's work an example using this formula to calculate the reliability of interval recording. Let's say that two observers record a behavior for 50 10-second intervals. Both observers agree on the occurrence of behavior in 20 intervals, disagree in 5 intervals, and neither records any occurrence of behavior in the remaining 25 intervals. The reliability would be 80% calculated by:

Percentage of Agreement = $\dfrac{20}{20 + 5}$ = 80%

Those 25 intervals in which neither observer recorded an occurrence of the behavior are not used in the computation.

GRAPHING OBSERVATIONAL DATA

After observers have gathered data they usually incorporate the data into a graph. The old adage "a picture is worth a thousand words" holds true. By converting the data into a graph we can see the changes that occur over time.

A line graph, which shows the relationship between two or more variables, is used to "picture" the data. Time, which may be represented in seconds, minutes, days, weeks, and so on, is placed along the horizontal axis of the graph. Frequency, duration, or percentage is represented along the vertical axis. Then, each point on the graph represents the occurrence of the behavior for the given time period.

The usual convention for graphing the data is illustrated in Figure 6.1.

Once we plot the data it is important for us to look at the graph to examine the trend. The trend can be stable, increasing, decreasing, or variable. A stable trend is one in which the frequency, duration, or percentage remains relatively constant for three to five time periods. An increasing trend is one in which the frequency, duration, or percentage is

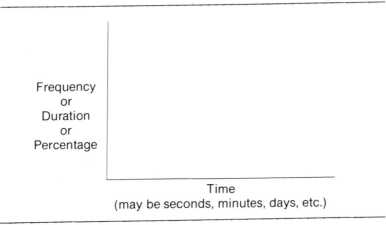

Figure 6.1 Format for Graphing Data

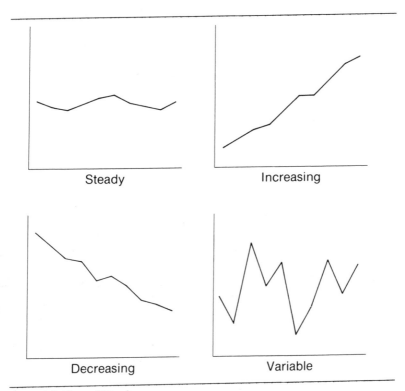

Figure 6.2 Type of Trends

ascending with time, while a decreasing trend is one in which the trend is moving downward. A variable trend is one where the frequency, duration, or percentage is fluctuating within upper and lower bounds. Examples of these trends are shown in Figure 6.2.

DESIGNS

In the beginning of this chapter we said that the purpose of single subject research is to see if there is a change in behavior and to determine if our intervention is responsible for that change. Graphing the data allows us to see if there has been a change in behavior. In order to determine if our intervention was responsible for that change, we must employ a research design.

Our discussion will be limited to simple single case research designs. In these designs, the dependent variable or behavior is monitored continuously before, during, and after intervention. The periods of monitoring before and after intervention are called baseline or "A" phases. The "B" phase is the period of monitoring during the intervention.

By using combinations of baseline (A) and intervention (B) phases we can construct a number of designs. The three most common designs are the AB design, the reversal and withdrawal designs (ABAB), and the multiple-baseline design.

AB DESIGN

The AB design is the most basic of the single subject designs. This design consists of a baseline (A) followed by a period of intervention (B). Baseline information is gathered until there is a satisfactory estimate of the frequency, duration, or percentage of occurrence of the behavior. Once the baseline information is collected, then the treatment is introduced. Information about the behavior continues to be gathered throughout the intervention phase. All of the information is plotted on a graph that shows the occurrence of the behavior during the baseline and the treatment phases.

An AB design was used by a human service worker to evaluate the effectiveness of a clinical program to reduce compulsive hand washing by a client named Mary. The worker asked Mary to record the number of times she washed her hands each day, for seven days. These

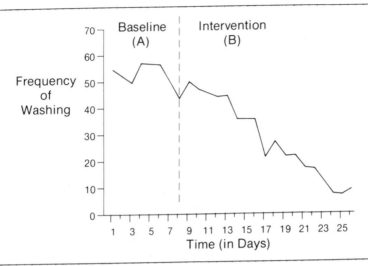

Figure 6.3   Example of the AB Design

recordings served as the baseline or "A" phase of the research design. After therapy began Mary continued to record the number of times that she washed her hands each day. This represented the "B" or intervention phase. The data were then graphed to see if hand washing had decreased (Figure 6.3).

The AB design is useful because it can be used in most treatment situations and settings. It provides for a data-based comparison of the behavior before and after treatment. However, there is a basic problem with the design. Even though there is a clear increase or decrease in the behavior during the intervention phase we cannot say for certain that the change was caused by the treatment.

For example, in the case of Mary, she could have reduced the frequency of washing her hands because they became so sore that it was too painful for her to be constantly washing them. Perhaps Mary found another job in which she kept so busy that she did not have time to wash her hands. Also, Mary could have become so embarrassed by the way her hands looked that she stopped washing them so often. The point is that many things could have accounted for the decline in her hand-washing behavior and the AB design does not allow us to conclude absolutely that the decline was due to the therapy or treatment. For this reason, the AB design is considered to be a relatively weak design. Nevertheless, it is useful when no other designs are feasible.

In addition, the strength of this design can be increased by repeating or *replicating* the "A" and "B" phases with additional clients. For example, if the worker's treatment was successful in reducing compulsive hand washing in a number of clients in addition to Mary, our confidence would be increased that it was in fact the treatment (and not some other factor) that caused the reduction in hand washing.

REVERSAL AND
WITHDRAWAL DESIGNS (ABAB)

The reversal and withdrawal designs consist of a baseline (A), followed by intervention (B), a return to baseline (A), and a reapplication of the intervention (B). The logic behind these designs is that if the treatment is responsible for the change in behavior, then the behavior should return to pretreatment levels when the treatment is withdrawn or reversed. If this does happen, then other possible causes for the change in behavior could be ruled out. Thus ABAB designs overcome the major weakness of the AB design.

Although many researchers do not distinguish between reversal and withdrawal designs, Leitenberg (1973) pointed out an important difference. In the withdrawal design a treatment is *withdrawn* in the third phase (A). In the reversal design, during the third phase the same treatment is applied to an alternative, but incompatible, behavior. In both cases, however, the target behavior is expected to return to baseline levels in the third phase.

An example of a reversal design can be seen in the case of John, a caseworker at a shelter for the homeless. The workers at the shelter noticed that John interacted a great deal with other staff and spent little time with clients. The workers felt that they contributed to John's behavior by giving him attention and engaging in conversations with him. They decided on a plan to increase John's interaction with clients. The treatment consisted of shortening their conversations with him or, if possible, ignoring him when he approached them. They also decided to praise him verbally when he interacted with clients. Baseline was established and the treatment was introduced. Then, treatment was withdrawn and later reintroduced. The staff recorded the amount of time that John spent interacting with clients and the time that he spent interacting with them. These data are presented in Figure 6.4.

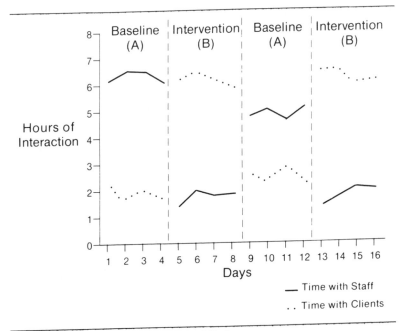

Figure 6.4   Example of the ABAB Reversal Design

The situation of Jill, a social worker, illustrates the withdrawal design. Jill always arrived late for meetings and appointments. She wanted to change this behavior, so she decided to use herself as a subject in her own study. She monitored her behavior for one week by recording the number of minutes she was late for meetings and appointments (baseline). During the next week she rewarded herself at the end of each day in which her tardiness had decreased (intervention). Her reward consisted of engaging in an enjoyable activity at the end of the day such as eating dinner at a restaurant, playing tennis, or going to a movie. During the third week she did not reward herself (baseline), while during the fourth week she once again engaged in enjoyable activities when she had reduced the amount of time she was late (intervention). As seen in Figure 6.5, her rewards caused her tardiness to meetings and appointments to diminish.

There are numerous variations of the ABAB design that can be employed depending on the particular research situation. Hersen and Barlow (1976) provide the following examples:

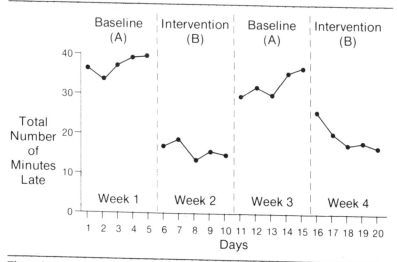

Figure 6.5 Example of the ABAB Withdrawal Design

A-B-A-B-A-B

A-B-A-C-A-C-A where B = Treatment 1 (e.g., feedback) and C = Treatment 2 (e.g., token reinforcement)

A-B-A-B-B'-B''-B''' where B, B', B'', and B''' = varying amounts of something (e.g., free play time allowed)

A-B-A-B-BC where B = Treatment 1, C = Treatment 2, and BC = A Combination of Treatment 1 and Treatment 2 given simultaneously

A-B-BC-BCD where B = Treatment 1, C = Treatment 2, D = Treatment 3, BC = Treatment 1 and Treatment 2 given simultaneously and BCD = Treatment 1, Treatment 2, and Treatment 3 given simultaneously

A major limitation to using reversal and withdrawal designs is that it is not always possible to stop treatment to see if the behavior returns to baseline levels. In many cases it would be unethical to withdraw the treatment. This would be the case, for instance, if the behavior under treatment was self-injury by an autistic child. If the injurious behavior were unsuccessfully reduced in the first treatment phase it would be unethical to allow it to return to its original level during the second baseline.

Another limitation of withdrawal and reversal designs is that they are not suitable for evaluating the effect of a treatment on behaviors that cannot be reversed. For example, assume that a treatment program increases the level of reading accomplishment in the first treatment phase. Since reading comprehension cannot be unlearned, it will not be possible to reestablish baseline in this study. This makes it impossible to evaluate the effectiveness of the treatment in this instance. A more appropriate design, such as the multiple-baseline design (described below) should be used to evaluate the effect of treatment on behaviors that cannot be reversed.

MULTIPLE-BASELINE DESIGNS

Multiple-baseline designs utilize the AB format—baseline followed by intervention. However, the AB design is repeated by applying the intervention to two or more behaviors, subjects, or settings. In this design baseline is established for a number of behaviors, subjects, or settings and then the treatment is systematically applied to one behavior, subject, or setting at a time.

The logic of the multiple-baseline design is that if the treatment is effective, each behavior (subject or setting) should respond only when the treatment is applied to that specific behavior. All other behaviors (subjects or settings) should remain at baseline levels until the treatment is applied.

Multiple-baseline designs are used in place of reversal and withdrawal designs where treatment is irreversible, as in the case where a client has learned a new behavior that cannot be unlearned. (This was the case in the reading comprehension example discussed above.) Multiple-baseline designs are also used when it is ethically impossible to stop treatment in order to return to baseline, for example, when treatment has reduced a client's self-destructive behavior.

A limitation of the multiple-baseline design is that the treated behaviors must be independent. Otherwise the specific effect of treatment on each behavior cannot be demonstrated. This is also true of multiple-baseline designs across settings and subjects. The settings must be independent, with no carryover from one setting to the other, and each subject's behavior must be unaffected by other subjects. In addition, it is assumed that the subjects are being exposed to similar environmental conditions.

The use of a multiple-baseline design across settings is illustrated by the treatment of Jane, an unassertive high school student who rarely

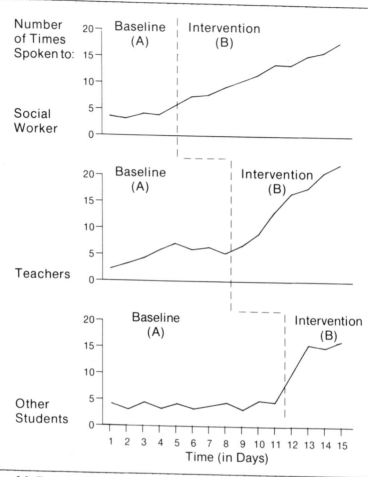

Figure 6.6 Example of a Multiple-Baseline Design Across Settings

spoke to students or teachers. Jane was also nearly silent with the school social worker.

The worker designed an assertiveness training program that used guided instruction, role playing, and praise to help Jane increase the number of times she spoke to others. With careful instruction from the worker Jane learned to record the frequency of her verbalizations. Since the worker was least threatening to Jane, the treatment program began with praise and directions to speak to the social worker. Later the treatment program was applied to "speaking with teachers," and, finally, "speaking to other students." Jane monitored her talking with the worker, teachers, and students throughout the program. The data are graphed in Figure 6.6.

An example of a multiple baseline across behaviors can be seen in the case of a 14-year-old girl named Kathy. Kathy's negative behaviors included hitting her siblings, cursing, and coming home late after school. After a stable baseline was established for each behavior, an intervention was introduced to address the hitting behavior. One week later the intervention was introduced to address her cursing and then after another week the intervention addressed the third behavior, coming home late after school. The intervention consisted of applying techniques that the parents had learned in a course on Parent Effectiveness Training that they had just completed. The parents monitored each of these behaviors and recorded the number of times Kathy hit her siblings, the number of times she cursed, and the number of minutes that she came home late from school. The multiple-baseline design across behaviors showed that the frequency of each of these behaviors decreased as the intervention was applied.

A multiple-baseline across subjects design was used to determine the effectiveness of a special program of mother-child interaction on the attention span of preschoolers in a nursery school. Jimmy's mother was taught special techniques to increase Jimmy's attention span. Several days later these techniques were taught to Mary's mother, who began to implement them. The techniques were then implemented sequentially with the other mothers in the program. Trained observers monitored all the children's attention spans in the classroom before the program, and continuously as each mother-child pair began the program.

The multiple-baseline design across subjects (children) showed that each child's classroom attention span increased only after the in-home training program began for that child. This was evidence that the training program was responsible for the increased classroom attention spans of the children.

SUMMARY

Single subject designs offer the practitioner/researcher a practical methodology to test the effectiveness of an intervention. They allow us to examine if there was a change in behavior and if our intervention was responsible for the change.

To answer these questions we must be able to monitor behavior. Monitoring includes measuring the frequency, duration, or percentage of occurrence of the behavior. We must also test the consistency of our observations. To do this another observer makes independent observations and the reliability of the observations is calculated by computing the percentage of agreement between the two observers.

Single subject designs for research begin with a baseline phase (A) followed by an intervention phase (B). Depending on the nature of the study, a variety of baseline and intervention phases can be employed. The most common single subject designs are the AB, the reversal and withdrawal, and the multiple baseline. Data about the behavior are graphed to demonstrate if any change occurred, and, if so, to determine whether our intervention was responsible for that change.

CASE STUDY

Single-Case Research Design

Carstensen, L. L., & Erickson, R. J. (1986). Enhancing the social environments of elderly nursing home residents: Are high rates of interaction enough? *Journal of Applied Behavior Analysis, 19*(4), 349-355.

This study utilized a reversal design to validate a commonly held belief that serving food during an activity at a nursing home would facilitate interaction among residents. The researchers postulated that serving refreshments consisting of unsweetened apple juice and plain butter cookies during a social hour at a nursing home would result in increased rates of social interaction among the residents. It was expected that the quality of social interaction would improve as well. This would be indicated by an increase in the number of positive statements made by the residents during the social hour and the positive statements reciprocated by their peers.

The nursing home had 32 residents. Of these, 30 participated in the study (one was out of the facility during the social hour and another was too ill to participate). There were 5 male and 25 female residents and their ages ranged from 55 to 97 years.

Carstensen and Erickson considered interaction to have occurred "when one or more subjects made eye contact with another subject for 0.5 s [seconds] or more with the torso and/or shoulders oriented toward that subject. Audible sounds and/or lip movements as well as nonvocal behaviors when there was physical contact, gesturing, or emotional facial expression in the presence of another subject, were considered interactions." With this definition it was not necessary for the resident to whom the interaction was directed to respond for the behavior to be considered an interaction. Interactions were distinguished from one another when there was a period of noninteraction lasting for 10 seconds or longer. Only resident-to-resident interactions were included in the analysis of this study.

Observations were made by two trained observers during each social hour. They collected data 5 days a week over a period of 5 weeks for 20 minutes a day during the social hour, which occurred between 3:30 and 4:30 pm. For purposes of monitoring, the two observers divided the subjects into two equal groups before entering the activity area, and then situated themselves closest to the residents they were to observe. The observers recorded each interaction that had occurred by repeating verbatim what they had heard into a tape recorder. If the interaction was not heard or understandable, then the observers said "inaudible interaction" into the recorder. When a resident would speak to an observer, the observer would say, "I cannot talk to you now; I will talk to you later." This minimized interactions with the observers.

To check the reliability of the observations, an independent observer recorded all interactions during 5-minute periods twice a week. This observer stood behind a wooden partition and was not visible to the principal observers. She recorded her observations in writing so that the principal observers would not hear her and be alerted that an observation was being recorded. The interobserver reliability was 100% for the recordings of the number of residents in attendance during each observational period. Consistency of the tape recorded observations with those made in writing by the independent observer was 99% using a percentage agreement statistic (i.e., the number of agreements between observers divided by the total number of observations made by either observer, multiplied by 100).

For each day of the study, the researchers computed two dependent variables: the number of patients in attendance at the activity, and the number of patient interactions. The study followed an ABAB reversal design. It consisted of a baseline phase with no refreshments (Baseline

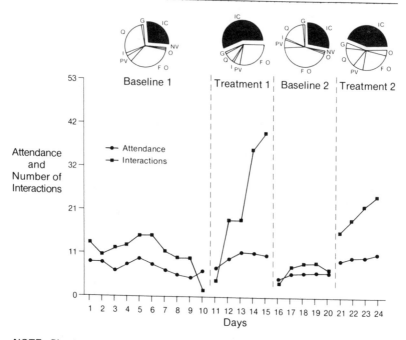

NOTE: Pie charts illustrate the breakdown by percentage of vocal content during each phase. IC = ineffective communication, NV = negative vocals, O = other, F/O = facts/opinions, PV = positive vocals, I = instructions, Q = questions, and G = greetings.

Figure 6.7   Frequency of Attendance and Number of Social Interactions During Baseline 1, Treatment 1, Baseline 2, and Treatment 2

1), serving refreshments to the residents (Treatment 1), a reversal condition with no refreshments (Baseline 2), and refreshments once again being served (Treatment 2). The duration of each phase varied, with Baseline 1 lasting for 10 days, Treatment 1 for 5 days, Baseline 2 for 5 days, and Treatment 2 for 4 days (Figure 6.7).

The procedure for serving the refreshments consisted of an attendant passing juice and cookies to the residents at the beginning of the observational period and once again 15 minutes later. All residents were asked if they would like to have some juice and a cookie. After serving the refreshments the attendant left the activity area and only returned at the time of the second serving. If residents spoke to the attendant while refreshments were being served, to minimize interaction, the attendant would respond by saying, "I cannot talk to you now; I have to get some more juice."

All of the tape recordings were transcribed verbatim. Two independent raters, who were blind to the purpose of the study, classified the transcriptions. The raters categorized the vocal behavior according to its content. With 20 possible codes available for classification, the vocal behaviors fell into eight categories—positive vocal (e.g., praise, compliments), negative vocal (e.g., reprimands, discouragement, derogatory remarks), facts/opinions, questions, greetings, instructions, ineffective communication (i.e., communications that were incoherent or nonsensical in content and directed toward another resident who did not responded to it), and other (e.g., singing). If there was a discrepancy between the classifications of the two raters, then a third rater was asked to evaluate the content.

This study used a single case design to modify conclusions that had been drawn from earlier studies of social interactions in nursing homes. Earlier studies showed that when refreshments were served during a social hour, residents interacted with each other more frequently. These studies were interpreted to mean that serving refreshments led to an increased quality of life for nursing home residents.

Carstensen and Erickson decided to look at this interpretation more closely. They replicated earlier studies by applying a reversal design to study the effects of refreshments on social interaction of nursing home residents. But they added an element to their design: In addition to monitoring frequency of interactions, they also recorded the *types* of interactions exhibited by residents. Their results were surprising (Figure 6.7).

As in the earlier studies, there was an increase in interactions when refreshments were served. But most of the increase was in *ineffective* communication: nonsensical or inappropriate statements or mumbling. In addition, during the refreshment-high-interaction phases (Treatment 1 and 2 in Figure 6.7), more appropriate interactions, such as questions, praise, and positive feedback, actually decreased.

The implication is clear: Simply increasing the frequency of interactions among nursing home residents does not ensure that those interactions will be meaningful. If we are to increase the quality of life in nursing homes, we need to attend to *how* residents interact with one another. Single case designs are useful ways to study social interactions if we use them to study both the quantity and the quality of human interaction.

Chapter 7

PROGRAM EVALUATION

Definition: *Program evaluation* is a type of research that uses established social science research methods (such as those discussed in this book) to evaluate the success or impact of a social service *program*.

It is useful to state what program evaluation is *not*. It is not "pure" or theoretical research, which has the goal of developing hypotheses and evaluating and creating theories. While the aim of pure research is to create knowledge for its own sake, evaluation research is always concerned with a program that serves people. That program may be in operation or it may be planned. But the results of program evaluation are always intended to be *applied* to a real world program.

Program evaluation differs from clinical evaluation in the target or intended beneficiary of the research. Clinical evaluation is a type of research used to evaluate small-scale interventions applied to individuals, families, and small groups. Research into the effectiveness of psychotherapy is the most common type of clinical evaluation.

Program evaluation may be used to answer the following types of questions:

(1) Does a job training program result in greater employment for trainees? Do trainees also obtain more skilled and higher paying jobs as a result of participating in the program?
(2) Does a program to provide in-home services (such as homemaking, chore and errand service, and telephone reassurance) to the noninstitu-

tionalized frail elderly prevent or delay placement into a nursing home? If so, are in-home services less expensive than nursing home care?

(3) Does establishment of a Regional Trauma Center in a local hospital result in fewer deaths and better medical care for traumatically injured community residents?

(4) Does a public education program about child sexual abuse reduce the incidence of this type of abuse?

As we saw in Chapters 5 and 6, every research endeavor uses some type of research design. Theoretically, every design discussed in those chapters can be used with any of the types of research: pure research, clinical research, and program evaluation.

In practice, it is more often possible for the first two types of research to use rigorous designs, that is, designs that use control groups and randomization procedures. Pure research and clinical research are typically conducted in controlled settings such as a psychology clinic or university lab, where the researcher is able to select individuals randomly and assign them to comparison groups. The researcher also has better control over the timing and circumstances of measurement, for example, the administration of intelligence tests or marital satisfaction surveys.

The program evaluator, on the other hand, is out in the real world where he or she often has little control over these factors. The program evaluator may be working with data that have been collected by others for other purposes (e.g., traffic fatality or birth data). Or he or she may be working within an agency, with staff who are more interested in providing services than in evaluating them.

For these reasons, program evaluations typically use "preexperimental" or "quasi-experimental" designs that are approximations to the experimental designs described in Chapter 5 of this book. Perhaps the most common research design in program evaluations is the One Group Pretest Posttest design described in Chapter 6. In this design a group is studied before and after an intervention. For example, a company may monitor the smoking of its employees before and after a campaign of incentives to stop smoking.

In recent years, with increasing public demands for accountability, governmental and agency researchers have been given the resources to evaluate programs with more rigorous designs.

For example, through the use of Medicaid waivers the federal government has made it possible to study the effectiveness of in-home services in preventing or delaying the placement of frail older persons in nursing homes. In a number of such program evaluations, researchers were able to use experimental designs by randomly assigning older persons to receive in-home services or to receive only routine services. The status of all participants was then tracked over time to see if those who received in-home services were less likely to be placed in nursing homes.

(By the way, the results of this research indicated that frail elderly who received in-home services used fewer days of hospital and nursing home care, but it is not clear if in-home maintenance is always less costly than nursing home care.) (Applebaum, Seidl, & Austin, 1980).

Although program evaluation often differs from other forms of research in the types of research designs used, all forms of research share a common purpose. They all seek to answer questions by using established social science research methodologies as described in this book. Use of these methodologies helps to ensure that answers to our research questions are valid and reliable, whether they apply to individuals, families, groups, communities, or programs.

TYPES OF PROGRAM EVALUATION

Suchman (1967) suggested that program evaluation be classified into five types. Each type corresponds to a different criterion that can be used to evaluate a program:

- effort
- performance
- impact or adequacy of performance
- efficiency
- process

Effort. Effort evaluations ask, "What did you do?" and "To what extent did you do it?" Effort evaluations study the quantity and extent of the interventions that make up the program.

We might, for example, implement a program to increase public awareness of abuse of the elderly. At a very minimum our funding source will expect us to provide data on our *effort.* An effort evaluation would record and present the following data: dollars expended on print, radio, and television advertising; number of educational workshops provided for professionals who come into contact with the elderly (this will include the numbers who attended); the number of calls handled by a toll-free Abuse Reporting telephone service established as part of the program; the number of leaflets and brochures distributed through the mail and at community meetings; and the number of families that utilized senior day care services (a preventive measure).

It should be clear from this example that effort evaluations tell us nothing about the *effectiveness* of our program. In the past, funding agencies were often satisfied with effort data alone. Today, most funding sources will also require research to document results as well as effort. This is done through the next type of evaluation.

Performance. Performance evaluation measures results rather than efforts. While an effort evaluation is a useful first step, it is the performance evaluation that tells us if our goals were actually met.

In the above example, our long-term goal is to reduce elder abuse. Our performance evaluation would gather data on subgoals such as these:

- How many additional cases (if any) of elder abuse were reported?
- In how many of the reported cases was the abuse effectively stopped?
- How many abusers were successfully prosecuted?
- In how many instances of reported abuse was the older person required to relocate? What was the impact of this relocation on the well-being of the older person?

Ultimately, we want to assess, "Has the actual incidence of elder abuse diminished in our community?"

Obtaining performance data in addition to effort data is crucial to program evaluation, because successful effort does not ensure successful performance. In this example, the prevention program of advertising, workshops, and so on may not alter the actual incidence of elder abuse. Increased public awareness of the problem may in fact have a contrary effect in that it may cause family members to hide the abuse more effectively.

This does not mean that our program was useless. It may simply mean that other, more effective methods must be employed to address the problem.

Most comprehensive program evaluations involve more than one type of evaluation. Effort and performance evaluations are used to

	No. Exposed to Program	Performance (Rate of Effectiveness)	Impact (No. Influenced)
Intensive Casework Program	100	50%	50
Public Education Program	10,000	10%	1000

Figure 7.1 Comparison of the Impact of Two Programs on Reducing Elder Abuse

answer the questions, "What did we do?" and "What results did it have?" These evaluations often precede the next type of program evaluation.

Impact or adequacy of performance. This type of program evaluation asks, "How effective is the program in meeting its goals, relative to the total amount of need?"

This question is important, because an effective program (i.e., one that meets the performance criterion) may have little impact on a behavior or social problem, unless the program is able to influence a sufficiently large number of people in the community. For example, this might happen in the following instance.

Human service workers have argued that disturbed family relationships are often at the bottom of elder abuse. Adult caretakers may themselves have been abused by the elderly parent that they are now abusing, and family conflicts rooted in early family life can be reactivated by the stress of caring for a dependent older parent. Caretakers may feel that the family has unfairly forced them into that role, and the resulting resentment then expresses itself as abuse of the older person.

Given the importance of family dynamics in causing elder abuse, one agency designed an intensive family casework program to reduce the likelihood of abuse. The program was very successful for the families that were served.

An impact evaluation, however, revealed that the program was not successful on the community level. The program was effective for the families it served. But since the agency was able to implement the program with only a limited number of families, the impact of the program on reducing elder abuse in the community was diminished. This is illustrated in Figure 7.1.

Figure 7.1 summarizes the results of the impact evaluation. Intensive casework is an effective intervention. But for the purpose of reducing elder abuse, a less potent campaign of public education is more adequate because it influences a larger number of people.

Efficiency. Efficiency evaluations assess the costs of implementing a program. Two types of questions are addressed by efficiency evaluations: (1) Do the benefits of implementing the program justify its costs? and (2) Are there alternative, less costly methods that will achieve the same results?

A technique called cost-benefit analysis is typically used to answer the first question. This is a purely economic procedure, in which dollar values are assigned to various costs and benefits. Then, total costs are divided into total benefits. If the ratio is greater than 1, this indicates that benefits outweigh costs.

Health economists have used cost-benefit analysis to evaluate the effect of universal national health insurance. The costs are primarily the dollar value of health insurance premiums to be paid by individuals, employers, and government. The benefits include the dollar value of reduced number of sick days, savings from improved coordination of services, and so on.

Cost-benefit analysis is not as scientific as it appears at first. There is a great deal of subjectivity in deciding what will be included as costs and benefits. Nevertheless, it is a useful tool for evaluating the economic efficiency of a program and determining whether a program should be initiated or continued.

Since there is almost always more than one way—or one program—to achieve a single goal, the second efficiency question is also important: Are there alternative, less costly methods that will achieve the same results?

For example, federally funded school lunch programs have been widely used to improve nutrition among low-income children. However, effort and performance evaluations have revealed many problems with the program: inefficient food purchasing that results in high costs relative to local supermarket prices, disposal of large quantities of ordered food because of poor planning, and unappetizing menus resulting in low student consumption (Lash & Sigal, 1976).

An efficiency evaluation of the school lunch program would compare the relative costs of more than one method to ensure adequate nutrition among low-income youth. Such an evaluation might find that expansion of the Food Stamp program or increasing AFDC (Aid to Families with

Dependent Children) grants, results in the same level of nutrition at lower cost.

Process. The types of evaluation discussed so far tell us if our program was implemented as planned, if it was effective, adequate, and efficient. These criteria determine the success of our program.

But, in addition to knowing whether our program was successful, it is often useful to know *why* it was or was not successful. That is the purpose of process evaluation.

A process evaluation assesses the components of a program to identify which ones contributed to its success and which did not. It traces the history of the program and the implementation of its various features to give us an understanding of what happened.

For example, imagine that the State Department on Aging implements a statewide Elder Abuse Hotline. Staffed by local volunteers, the purpose of the hotline is to encourage citizens to report suspected abuse, and to allow potential abusers to "let off steam" and find alternatives to abuse.

Assume that a program evaluation indicates the program is successful (as measured perhaps by a reduced incidence of older persons appearing in emergency rooms with suspicious injuries, fewer complaints filed with the nursing home ombudsman, and so on). It is also useful to know how and why the hotline led to a decrease in abuse.

A process analysis might show that the program was associated with decreased abuse, but only in urban and suburban areas. The incidence of abuse remains unchanged in rural areas of the state.

Further process analysis might reveal the reasons for this curious finding. Analysis of hotline records and interviews with rural service providers might reveal that rural citizens are less likely than their urban counterparts to use the hotline. Anonymity is the issue. Potential callers are dissuaded from calling because they may know the hotline volunteer or an acquaintance or relative of the volunteer. This sort of analysis is useful. In this case it would lead the program directors to institute and publicize new procedures to ensure caller anonymity.

NEEDS ASSESSMENT

Another type of research that is often helpful to program designers and evaluators is *needs assessment.* A needs assessment is a research and planning activity designed to determine human service needs and service utilization patterns.

Needs assessments are often useful in providing data for the establishment of new programs, or expansion of existing programs. For example, a needs assessment in a rural area found that many farmworker families experienced hunger before and after the harvest season. Although food surplus commodities were available, these were underutilized because of poor access to food distribution centers, shame associated with accepting in-kind assistance, and poor variety of available food. This needs assessment led to an outreach program to enlist more of these families in the Food Stamp program. Food Stamps are generally more acceptable to the poor; they can be used like cash to supplement the family's food budget and therefore allow for greater choice and selection of food items.

The evaluation of existing programs can also be enhanced by a needs assessment. In our Food Stamp example, continuation of the needs assessment will tell us if the Food Stamp Outreach Program results in greater program participation and less hunger.

According to Warheit, Bell, and Schwab (1979) there are five approaches for conducting a needs assessment. These include the key informant approach, the community forum approach, the rates-under-treatment approach, the social indicators approach, and the survey approach. These approaches can be used separately or in combination.

The *key informant* approach relies on information obtained from persons who are in the position of knowing a community's needs and service utilization patterns. Key informants are the kinds of individuals who are familiar with a community, its residents and their needs, and available services. These persons normally include public officials, clergy, physicians, social workers, and other staff and board members of agencies and organizations. Information is normally collected from key informants by interview or questionnaire.

The *community forum* approach is based on individuals coming together at public meetings and expressing their opinions about the needs and services of a community. This approach, like the key informant approach, relies on the impressions of persons who know the community. However, because the community forum approach utilizes public meetings, more of the general population can be involved and even specific groups—such as the elderly or ethnic minorities— can be targeted to provide testimony. To maximize the input and full participation of individuals, the public meetings are kept small in size.

Large assemblies are usually avoided because they are not conducive to the open exchange that is needed. At these meetings, the researcher records the ideas, attitudes, and opinions of participants. Later, a summary of all suggestions made regarding the needs and services is prepared, with priority areas noted.

The *rates-under-treatment* approach to needs assessment is based on descriptive characteristics gleaned from service utilization data. The underlying assumption is that the needs of a community can be determined by examining the needs of those who have received services. For example, if a home health agency finds that most of their cases consist of elderly individuals age 75 and older who live alone, then the agency can infer that this group is more in need than those who are younger and living with others. Agency records can often provide descriptive characteristics of their clientele (e.g., age, sex, race, income), the presenting problems of their clients, the types, frequency, and duration of the services they received, and the outcome of the services provided. This information, when compiled, can be valuable in establishing the need for services.

The *social indicators* approach relies on inferences made from descriptive information found in public records, documents, and reports. The assumption of this approach to needs assessment is that it is possible to estimate the needs of a community based on data that are known to be strong indicators of need. For example, if you were going to use the social indicators approach to estimate the need for a drug and alcohol program in a specific community, you could examine arrests related to drug and alcohol violations, the number of DUI (driving under the influence) offenses, the number of traffic accidents involving drugs or alcohol, coroner's reports that indicate the use of drugs or alcohol, the amount of beer and liquor sales within the community, hospital emergency room statistics, and so on. All these indicators, when taken together, give a good picture of the need for services.

The most rigorous method for conducting a needs assessment is the *survey approach*. This approach utilizes questionnaires or interview schedules to collect data from a sample or an entire population. It relies on many of the principles and methods for social science research that are discussed throughout this text. With the survey approach, subjects are asked to report on their problems, needs, and patterns of service utilization. For example, suppose an agency serving the elderly wants to find out if the needs of the elderly who reside in a new senior citizen high-rise are being met by the agency. The agency could conduct a needs assessment by interviewing all of the elderly residents in the building to examine their needs for, and utilization of, the services provided by the agency, including transportation, homemaker and chore services, meals-on-wheels, home health care, recreation and socialization programs, and case management. Using information gathered from the needs assessment, the agency could better tailor its services to clients.

SUMMARY

Program evaluation is like other types of human service research in that it uses established social science research methodology. It is distinguished by its focus on evaluating the success of social service programs. Because of the constraints of doing research in the real world, program evaluators must often use modifications of the more rigorous experimental designs. Programs are evaluated on the basis of one or more of the following criteria: effort, performance, impact or adequacy of performance, efficiency, and process. Needs assessments, aimed at determining human service needs and utilization patterns, can also be used to evaluate the need for, or the impact of, human service programs. Five approaches exist for conducting a needs assessment: key informant, community forum, rates-under-treatment, social indicators, and the survey approach.

RANDOM NUMBER TABLE

53706	22285	80527	52917	83170	61000	70742	24925	63365	77507
63848	17393	61768	72149	39081	65323	20995	07050	35757	17743
49794	68434	23328	35968	64105	12369	44054	10329	08839	19929
90016	10178	41106	40295	58710	96164	43461	65043	00759	90018
09736	13510	03995	17560	85072	54892	18712	48031	04448	42147
39497	71929	86048	89768	69874	41270	67419	52451	11370	31625
89115	97651	07196	43914	90402	01461	89910	73400	48587	22465
95773	49371	78114	80790	79650	88107	02218	87515	41451	03018
11707	37312	67035	08583	57289	72198	63455	11680	22850	88820
05771	32200	94306	77682	57601	37141	85135	43856	35195	51303
06791	60096	15902	61122	93508	32460	19749	23930	05464	85836
49506	49283	76273	17988	63809	09659	94585	59000	20134	76792
27518	95592	63431	19306	65614	12294	76115	28657	28665	60712
68439	03629	20333	93218	90361	46364	74320	87522	06047	22376
74828	89659	95799	51072	07087	81144	14884	14216	07181	28423
35153	23195	97394	88983	99290	81183	15243	62227	70968	92604
48634	82399	59382	51456	04912	03844	54950	46138	34393	48215
52597	66444	92752	85002	19123	99561	05333	61034	55327	15313
62037	07589	30631	68211	35632	87078	04638	68423	32331	18983
32282	82566	27174	21599	48405	04097	97354	38100	79198	75534
03116	15532	27695	97126	21216	90261	22127	24684	15037	59657
84320	22336	53634	00347	23652	49270	85431	93805	19619	63466
59902	82564	16047	72241	47055	67544	18282	98202	61147	82603
53989	19584	37741	39782	31311	57068	32521	00874	21436	61469
39771	54955	03622	47129	16284	63246	18504	10364	50555	54619
16990	10247	75400	01445	81637	00452	58598	55825	26661	86666
25223	62311	31067	02631	16098	56474	29011	62962	09203	15182
10778	19971	19853	73705	70162	14449	45306	54572	05208	47133
43770	56555	23578	62861	45140	90889	78076	93604	41554	88802
94006	18507	77401	59884	39787	53068	21099	61647	35416	58327
93900	88973	06933	49764	37608	92136	26326	82330	91341	45662
11107	63380	51549	78045	67709	22058	63634	99014	92169	79318
63468	03489	78317	52418	37335	56317	53415	38138	46737	80573
79565	72464	15472	83225	40253	82290	52678	13020	31744	90865
66341	58142	64681	84402	00463	01309	02106	83237	90154	00893
67205	87816	35226	20020	01754	85895	46393	45336	27038	23093
19730	10171	63972	82265	89081	91651	24210	66749	48405	45019
84139	80212	99510	64787	40432	24319	10354	57376	26341	87082
88652	14588	61513	27100	25232	80356	88968	64195	87541	88248
41917	21970	64809	82897	09464	42183	12577	41783	69774	62085
96519	32713	81681	37556	86646	35147	05451	01030	69605	48538
93963	16862	57638	83267	29095	92588	10446	74698	15760	77471
10976	75246	39956	95737	59958	90498	17237	60906	07561	37932

SOURCE: Copyright 1987: Raymond M. Berger, California State University, Long Beach.

REFERENCES

Aldous, J. (1986). Cuts in selected welfare programs: The effects on U.S. families. *Journal of Family Issues, 7*(2), 161-177.

Applebaum, R., Seidl, F. W., & Austin, C. D. (1980, June). The Wisconsin Community Care Organization: Preliminary findings from the Milwaukee Experiment. *Gerontologist, 20*(3), 350-355.

Atherton, C. R., & Klemmack, D. L. (1982). *Research methods in social work.* Lexington, MA: D. C. Heath.

Baltes, P. B., & Labouvie, G. J. (1973). Adult development of intellectual performance: Description, explanation, and modification. In C. Eisdorfer & M. P. Lawton (Eds.), *The psychology of adult development and aging.* Washington, DC: American Psychological Association.

Berger, R. M. (1984). *Gay and gray: The older homosexual man.* Boston: Alyson. Reprinted from Urbana-Champaign: University of Illinois Press, 1982.

Berger, R. M. (1986, January). A better recipe for social work practice models. *Social Casework, 67*(1), 45-54.

Berger, R. M., & Piliavin, I. (1976a, May). The effects of casework: A research note. *Social Work, 21*(3), 205-208.

Berger, R. M., & Piliavin, I. (1976b, September). A rejoinder by Berger and Piliavin. *Social Work, 21*(5), 349ff.

Bieber, I. (1965). Clinical aspects of male homosexuality. In J. Marmor (Ed.), *Sexual inversion: The multiple roots of homosexuality* (pp. 248-267). New York: Basic Books.

Blenkner, M., Bloom, M., & Nielsen, M. (1971, October). A research and demonstration project of protective services. *Social Casework, 52*(8), 483-499.

Botwinick, J. (1978). *Aging and behavior* (2nd ed.). New York: Springer.

Bourne, L. E., Jr., & Ekstrand, B. R. (1982). *Psychology: Its principles and meanings* (4th ed.). New York: Holt, Rinehart & Winston.

Campbell, D. T., & Stanley, J. C. (1963). *Experimental and quasi-experimental designs for research.* Chicago: Rand-McNally.

Carstensen, L. L., & Erickson, R. J. (1986) Enhancing the social environments of elderly nursing home residents: Are high rates of interaction enough? *Journal of Applied Behavior Analysis, 19*(4), 349-355.

Deimling, G. T., & Bass, D. M. (1986). Symptoms of mental impairment among elderly adults and their effects on family caregivers. *Journal of Gerontology, 41*(6), 778-784.

Drew, C. J. (1980). *Introduction to designing and conducting research* (2nd. ed.). St. Louis: C. V. Mosby.

Edinberg, M. A. (1985). *Mental health practice with the elderly.* Englewood Cliffs, NJ: Prentice-Hall.

Freud, S. (1920). *A general introduction to psychoanalysis.* New York: Liverright.

Goldfarb, A. I. (1962, January). Prevalence of psychiatric disorder in metropolitan old age and nursing homes. *Journal of the American Geriatrics Society, 10*(1), 77-84.

Hershen, M., & Barlow, D. H. (1976). *Single case experimental designs.* New York: Pergamon.

Homans, G. C. (1965). Group factors in worker productivity. In H. Proshansky & L. Seidenberg (Eds.), *Basic studies in social psychology* (pp. 592-604). New York: Holt.

Jirovec, R. (1984). Documenting the impact of Reaganomics on social welfare recipients. *Arete, 9*(1), 36-47.

Joint Commission on Mental Illness and Health. (1961). *Action for mental health.* New York: Science Editions.

Julian, J., & Kornblum, W. (1983). *Social problems* (4th ed.). Englewood Cliffs, NJ: Prentice-Hall.

Kerlinger, F. N. (1973). *Foundations of behavioral research* (2nd ed.). New York: Holt, Rinehart & Winston.

Lash, T. W., & Sigal, H. (1976). *State of the child: New York City.* New York: Foundation for Child Development.

Leitenberg, H. (1973). The use of single-case methodology in psychotherapy research. *Journal of Abnormal Psychology, 82*(1), 87-101.

Macdonald, M. E. (1960). Social work research: A perspective. In N. A. Polansky (Ed.), *Social work research* (pp. 1-23). Chicago: University of Chicago Press.

McCain, G., & Segal, E. M. (1969). *The game of science* (2nd ed.). Belmont, CA: Brooks/Cole.

Patchner, M. A. (1982, spring). A decade of social work doctoral graduates: Their characteristics and educational programs. *Journal of Education for Social Work, 18*(2), 35-41.

Patchner, M. A. (1983a, winter). The experiences of DSWs and Ph.D.s. *Journal of Education for Social Work, 19*(1), 98-106.

Patchner, M. A. (1983b). The practitioner becomes a student: The stresses of transition. *Journal of Continuing Social Work Education, 2*(2), 21-23, 31.

Pincus, A., & Minahan, A. (1973). *Social work practice: Model and method.* Itasca, IL: Peacock.

President's Commission on Mental Health. (1978). *Report to the president* (Vol. 1). Washington, DC: Government Printing Office.

Rosenblatt, A., & Kirk, S. A. (1981, spring). Cumulative effect of research courses on knowledge and attitudes of social work students. *Journal of Education for Social Work, 17*(2), 26-34.

Rosenthal, R., & Jacobson, L. (1968). *Pygmalion in the classroom.* New York: Holt, Rinehart & Winston.

Schuster, C. S., & Ashburn, S. S. (1980). *The process of human development: A holistic approach.* Boston: Little, Brown.

Selltiz, C., Wrightsman, L. S., & Cook, S. W. (1976). *Research methods in social relations* (3rd ed.). New York: Holt, Rinehart & Winston.

Simon, B. K. (1970). Social casework theory: An overview. In R. W. Roberts & R. H. Nee (Eds.), *Theories of social casework*. Chicago: University of Chicago Press.

Stein, H. D. (1969). *The crisis in welfare in Cleveland*. Cleveland: Case Western Reserve University.

Suchman, E. A. (1967). *Evaluative research: Principles and practice in public service and social action programs*. New York: Russell Foundation.

Suppe, F. (1982). *Committee on the history and philosophy of science*. University of Maryland.

U.S. Congress, Joint Economic Committee, Subcommittee on Fiscal Policy. (1972). *Issues in welfare administration: Welfare—An administrative nightmare*. Washington, DC: Government Printing Office.

Warheit, G. J., Bell, R. A., & Schwab, J. J. (1979). *Needs assessment approaches: Concepts and methods*. Washington, DC: Government Printing Office.

Webster's new world dictionary of the American language. (1964). (College ed.). Cleveland: World Publishing.

Zimbalist, S. E. (1977). *Historic themes and landmarks in social welfare research*. New York: Harper & Row.

ABOUT THE AUTHORS

RAYMOND M. BERGER, ACSW, Ph.D., is Professor of Social Work at California State University, Long Beach, where he is Chair of the Research Sequence. He has taught research methods to social work students for more than 12 years. Widely published in social work and gerontology, he is listed in *International Authors and Writers Who's Who,* and has served on the editorial boards of *Social Work* and *Behavioral Group Therapy.*

MICHAEL A. PATCHNER, ACSW, Ph.D., is Associate Professor at the University of Illinois at Urbana—Champaign in the School of Social Work. He has taught courses on research methods, program and practice evaluation, and computer use for more than 10 years. He has worked in practice settings as a researcher and computer programmer and has administered a number of publicly funded research projects. He has been published extensively in the fields of social work and gerontology.